Do you know your

Guardian Angel?

Do you know your
Guardian Angel?

Unlock the secrets to a magical life

JACKY NEWCOMB

CICO BOOKS

LONDON NEW YORK

Published in 2015 by CICO Books
an imprint of Ryland Peters & Small Ltd
20-21 Jockey's Fields, London WC1R 4BW
341 E 116th St. New York NY 10029
www.rylandpeters.com

10 9 8 7 6 5 4 3 2 1

Text © Jacky Newcomb 2015
Design and illustrations © CICO Books 2015

A CIP catalog record for this book is available from the Library of Congress
and the British Library.

ISBN: 978-1-78249–262-7

Printed in China

Editor: Marion Paull
Designer: Emily Breen
Illustrator: Jane Taylor

Commissioning editor: Kristine Pidkameny
In-house editor: Dawn Bates
In-house designer: Fahema Khanam
Art director: Sally Powell
Head of production: Patricia Harrington
Publishing manager: Penny Craig
Publisher: Cindy Richards

Additional illustrations by Trina Dalziel:
pages 1, 13. 14 (t), 26, 37, 48, 58, 64, 76, 89, 95, 100

Contents

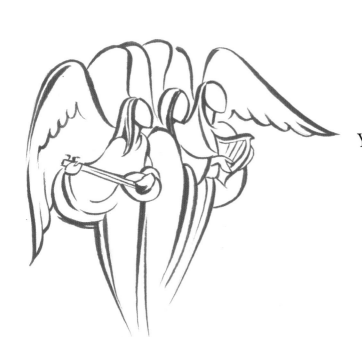

Introduction

I'm so happy to introduce this beautiful new book to you. Working with angels isn't hard, but I realize it's easier to do if you have a little inspiration to get you started. I know you'll feel motivated to connect with your own angels as you flick through the book.

I work a lot with a planner and notebook at home. It's true that if you write something down, you are far more likely to remember it. That was how I came up with the idea of a special section you can make your own. We create the book together!

I've included some fun exercises for you to complete … if you want to; and your very own journal section in which to record your answers. You may prefer to use pencil or search for a pretty pen with ink you can rub out—you'll be happier to fill in the sections and not worry too much if you make a mistake! Don't worry about spellings; no one else need read your notes. It's your own private resource (if someone else takes an interest, they can always buy their own copy!).

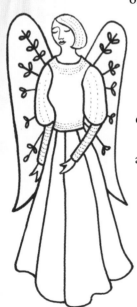

You might prefer to read the book all the way through first of all or pick out sections randomly. You don't have to complete the exercises in any particular order but fill them in if you feel excited to do so!

I hope you enjoy the true life stories. Why not keep a notebook to record your experiences if you run out of room? Use a ribbon or pretty headband to keep your notes and book together. Enjoy!

How I discovered angels

Did you grow up with the knowledge that you had a Guardian Angel? I know I did. I remember hearing about angels when I was at school and longing to be an angel in the nativity play. I was never asked to be one, though. I always worried about that. The angels were the most coveted of all the parts, even more so than the role of Mary!

Before that, I remember the angel on top of the Christmas tree. She was the most glamorous of all our home decorations, with her glued-on feather wings and her tinsel crown halo. My sisters and I always fought over who was to place her in prime position. I don't recall that it was ever me. My longing for angels in my life seems to have begun at a very young age.

I knew angels were beautiful, white, and sparkly. Angels looked after us and angels protected us. I think I always knew that, but were they real? Now, I was never too sure about that. Later, I remember reading about angels in the Bible at school. I'd seen gorgeous stained-glass windows in church depicting angels interacting with human souls and, in the grounds of the churchyard, little cherubs sitting on gravestones.

Angels were a subtle part of everyday life. They were always around in the background, carved into old buildings and occasionally decorating items for the home. Even though we were taught that they were real beings, it was something we had to believe in based on faith. In other words, we were told they were real but we were never offered any proof.

Yet even as a young girl I had strange and magical experiences that didn't fit what was classed as "normal." Things that happened to me did not always relate to the rules of life as I was taught. At times I felt guided or led. I felt warnings in dangerous situations and, on occasion, heard voices inside my head. I felt that "something" seemed distinct and separate from my own thoughts. Was this my Guardian Angel? I hoped so.

"Make yourself familiar with the Angels and behold them frequently in spirit; for without being seen, they are present with you."

St. Francis de Sales (Bishop of Geneva)

As an adult, I recalled some of my childhood experiences and wanted to discover if other people had lived this, too. Had my own occasionally paranormal happenings anything to do with angels, and, if so, was this the real proof I longed for? I recalled waking up in the night and seeing a being at the end of the bed. I recalled times when I'd felt sad or lonely and then felt as if an unknown presence had been with me.

With the birth of the Internet, everything became possible. I set up a website about angels, and people from all over the world began writing to me. These kindly people talked about their own experiences of angels, often confiding that they'd never shared what had happened to them for fear of being laughed at. In those days, mockery from non-experiencers was a real possibility. I was honored that these people trusted me.

What I'd longed for myself was proof that angels were real. I wanted to hear about truthful encounters with these majestic beings of light. I was excited to explore tales of true-life interaction, and then mesmerized as I

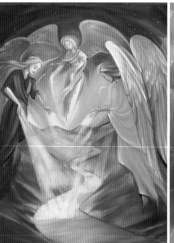

began to notice patterns and connections between one story and the next. People all over the world were having very similar experiences. People who had never met one another had experienced angels in their lives in very similar ways. I was convinced. Angels were real and it was such a relief!

My life mission was fixed. I instantly knew that my role was to document these angel experiences and spread the word. I planned to write a book of angel stories. I felt so excited by my new-found discovery, I wanted to tell everyone all about it. Imagine, I thought, how people's lives would be changed when they knew I had the proof they'd been looking for. Angels are real. Would folk be comforted, as I was? Would they be relieved, as I'd been? Would they feel the joy that I had felt?

That one book became two, then three, then four. Over the years, I've published piles of books about angels, and each one has been more amazing than the last. I've never lost my thirst for knowledge of these wonderful beings. The more we learn, the more we realize that there is so much more to know. In time I felt that connection grow. As I wrote about angels, I learned a little more. As I read about angels, I felt my own Guardian Angel draw closer.

Do you know your Guardian Angel? Let me share with you what I have learned. Throughout the book, for convenience, I've referred to angels as female but, of course, they can just as easily be male, although they often appear to be of no specific gender.

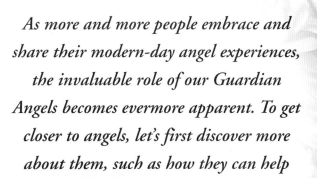

CHAPTER 1

What is a Guardian Angel?

As more and more people embrace and share their modern-day angel experiences, the invaluable role of our Guardian Angels becomes evermore apparent. To get closer to angels, let's first discover more about them, such as how they can help us and what they might look like.

Discovering Angels

The most popular description of angels is that they are beings of light, different from humans but created by God (our creator being, Goddess, or Source, or whatever you might call that highest of all energies). Some people believe they were created just before humankind and others that they were created just after.

We know that some angels have been specifically "birthed" by God to care for humankind, and this information comes to us via tradition (spoken-word stories passed on from one generation to the next), religious texts, ancient manuscripts, true-life experiences documented from history, and modern-day encounters recorded in books, magazines, and the Internet.

True-life angel encounters are popular topics of conversation today. You'll find information on the radio, in magazine-style television chat shows, and in the national press. I've been featured in many newspapers myself as well as in other media. Public interest in true-life stories never seems to end and it does mean we continue to learn.

I believe the best way to learn more about angels is for us to keep sharing our experiences—and, of course, to read about them.

Q. *What do we know of their role with humankind?*

A. The word "angel" means "messenger." We know little of their roles away from Earth, but on our own planet we know angels have been assigned to help us in our day-to-day lives. They take care of us. They watch over us and help to protect us. We have many documented cases of angels intervening in people's lives (both ancient and modern), and there are books full of angel stories.

They can help us when we get into difficulties and step in during genuine emergencies. Mostly, we've discovered that we have to give them permission to help us. They can intervene but not interfere. They can guide but not control. They can suggest ideas but not tell us what to do.

Angels can help with big problems and small. They like it most of all when we work things out for ourselves, but when we are stuck, they can give us little clues to move us forward. You can ask your own Guardian Angel to step in when you need a little guidance.

Q. *What do angels really look like?*

A. Descriptions of angels vary greatly, and it is their "loving and peaceful energy" that lets us know we are in their presence. As beings of light, they sometimes choose to show themselves as glowing or whitish figures. Some people describe very tall figures with a human-type form. They seem to have no gender, appearing as male/female combined. There would be no need for them to have human reproductive parts as they are created at the will of God and don't need to create angel babies! If God felt more angels were needed, no doubt he would create them.

They might wear shimmering gowns that seem to fade away at the bottom. No one ever notices their feet, if indeed they have any. They might have a particular glow around the head (shown in paintings as a halo). Some people see angels with wings like birds and to others they appear without any wings at all.

Traditionally, angels were depicted in more scary ways than we might recognize today. Some of the earliest depictions show them as giant creatures, creating awe and fear in those who see them. The great Archangel Metatron is said

to be covered with 365,000 pairs of eyes and a surprising 36 pairs of wings; he's also made of pure flame. The Archangel Ariel's name means "Lion of God," which gives a clue to his image, and the Bible tells us that the Archangel Gabriel has 140 pairs of wings.

Despite these variations, if you've seen or been in the company of angels, you know it. Yet there is maybe one comment to remember—we are told that angels can appear to us "disguised" if they choose to do so. Perhaps this is to ensure that we are kindly to everyone, just in case …

Q. *Lots of people call their deceased relatives their Guardian Angels. Can this be so?*

A. When humans pass over to the other side, they remain as souls rather than angels in the way we traditionally recognize them. Yet my books contain numerous stories that show our deceased loved ones can and do watch over us from the afterlife, but they don't have the powers that angels have.

Like angels, the deceased can visit us while we sleep (body asleep, mind awake and lucid). They can bring warnings, guiding us away from danger or giving us a strong urge to follow one route or another. On occasions when real hazards present themselves, people have heard the physical voice of a passed-over loved one, calling out to them in warning. It's unsure if these warnings come from loving souls or if they work alongside our Guardian Angels, who might use a familiar voice to reach out to us more quickly.

Over the years, I've collected many stories of the deceased visiting children in the family. Children are more open than adults to spontaneous contact from heaven. Grandparents, parents, and

brothers or sisters who have crossed through the light of the heavenly realms come back to reassure youngsters with such words as, "Don't worry, I'll be your Guardian Angel now. I'll always be with you." Have you ever had a visit from a loved one who has appeared as a surrogate Guardian Angel?

> *"The angel of the Lord encampeth round about them that fear him, and delivereth them."*
>
> *Psalm 34:7*

Q. *Do we know how many angels there are?*

A. The Hebrew language has no word for millions, so the Bible (Revelation 5:1) says that there are "thousands upon thousands, and ten thousand times ten thousand" angels. People who have experienced near death (whose bodies have been through clinical bodily death and been revived) occasionally describe

OUR LOVED ONES

Many of us have friends or relatives helping from the afterlife. This loving contact is distinct and separate from the help we receive from our personal Guardian Angels but is certainly no less important to us. Have you ever felt that a special loved one in heaven is watching out for you on Earth? Maybe a loved one promised to be a Guardian Angel for you after they passed over? Who would your human angels be and why? Fill in the section in Chapter 8 so that you can keep your precious memories safe.

large hosts of many thousands of angels in the heavenly realms, which they visited in their spirit body before being sent back to Earth once more.

We are told that, beside Guardian Angels, many other angels fulfill varied roles, and since numerous religions believe that we each have our very own Guardian Angel, then clearly there are more than enough angels for everyone! That's probably all we need to know.

Q. *Can some people see angels more than others?*

A. In my experience, most people don't "see" angels, not with their physical eyes anyway. Although it's rare, children are more likely than adults to see angels during their normal waking state. Adults mostly see angels when they are asleep or in an altered state of consciousness, such as while daydreaming, meditating, or being unconscious.

People who have witnessed angels may have seen them as humans who disappeared after speaking. An angel might be there to offer comfort during a time of extreme stress or during an illness, maybe when the person is on the verge of sleep or, more often, is just waking up. In this state, we find it easier to accept the "paranormal" aspect of the encounter, rather than having a heart-attack because of the shock of what we've just seen, which wouldn't be terribly helpful now, would it?

These things don't happen every day, of course. Although my books are filled with angel experiences, someone contributing a story may have had just one angelic encounter in her whole life. Don't feel sad if you haven't seen an angel. You're more likely to sense they are around, smell a beautiful scent, or just feel their love as they stand with you.

Q. *What is an Archangel?*

A. Archangels are mentioned in many ancient texts, especially religious ones. The word Archangel translates as the higher shining ones or higher guardians. They are the higher ranking angels, who are placed above the guardian angels (those angels who work directly with individual humans).

They do work with humankind but are mainly responsible for things relating to larger issues. They are less interested in individual needs and more accountable for areas of land, bodies of water, or other planets or dimensions.

We can ask for archangels to assist us if we need to. Some of them are connected to Earth, the more well known of the angels include Archangel Michael and Raphael.

Q. *Are the angels that worked with ancient people really the same beings that are working on earth today?*

They are—literally! Angels that were created by God do not live and die in the way that humans do. They are beings of light, omnipotent (with the will of God). Some sources say they were created just before humans and others that they were "birthed" just after.

They are light beings made by a spark from this divine energy and were created to serve "HIS" wishes. Many of these angels were formed to act as translators between this higher energy and us, human beings (and we suspect beings on other planets and in other realms of existence, including beings on our own planet, which our microscopes are unable to see at this time).

Their existence does not rely on a physical body that has a short lifespan, meaning the Archangel Michael you read about in the Bible is the same Archangel Michael that people experience in the modern-day world. Many people write and share stories where they've experienced the Great Michael rescue them in some way—children especially! Angels are real and not a myth.

Modern-day Angels
and How they Help Us

Traditionally, angels have stayed very much in the background, hidden from us. Many people didn't believe in angels and were quick to laugh at those who did.

Even 12–15 years ago, people were nervous about sharing their encounters with others. Sharing can sometimes take away the magic of the experience, for example, especially when others respond cynically. In the early days of my research, there were few places, if any, where you could read about real-life encounters with these celestial helpers. Nowadays this has changed. If you believe in angels, it's easy to find others who do, too; the Internet provides a wonderful platform for interaction with other believers. Many, like me, have social-media pages, such as Facebook and Twitter, where they regularly post information about Guardian Angels.

In 2011, an Associated Press-GfK poll found that nearly eight out of ten Americans believe in angels. In polls, such as that one, numbers do vary from country to country. Another poll back in 2006 suggested that 81 percent of people believe in angels. Similar polls conducted in the UK usually indicate a lower level, but it's usually around the 50-percent mark or more.

These days, people crowd into my angel talks and workshops. There is more openness about belief in angels. The number of angel experiencers also seems to have grown. It's as if the curtain that hides us from the higher realms has been pulled back a little, enabling us to glimpse these majestic creatures from time to time.

Their modern-day tasks have much to do with leading us to our earthly missions. As humans, we seem to be born to perform certain tasks, and many of these roles have to do with learning and teaching about what it is to be a spiritual being. Some of us have agreed to help others along the way, and our angels have stepped forward to light the path of our journey. Our angels ensure that we are guided to our learning destination. They make sure we are in the right place at the right time. Their mysterious roles are becoming more apparent.

FIRST ANGELS

When did you first hear about angels? Have friends introduced you to them or perhaps a television program or book made you want to learn more? Fill in the section in Chapter 8.

An angel saved my life in the car

"When I was working, I used to travel from my home at about 4.30am. This particular morning, the roads were very treacherous; snow had fallen heavily overnight. I'd already had a small accident as my car slowly skidded into one that was parked. Then, as I was nearing Rawtenstall, I put my foot on the brake but the car began to slide toward the other side of the road where a very large truck was fast approaching.

"I was convinced that my life was about to end because I couldn't see any way that I could possibly avoid the lorry. The only option that seemed open to me was to close my eyes and wait for the crash. But strangely, nothing happened, and when I opened my eyes, I discovered I'd come to a safe stop on the wrong side of the road. The lorry had managed to pass me without incident but I never worked out quite how that could have happened. I'm convinced that someone was watching over me that day and I'll be forever grateful that they saved my life."

Janet

When my eldest daughter and granddaughter were involved in a car crash earlier this year, I was terribly upset and very shocked. Luckily, despite the state of the car after the accident, no one was seriously hurt. Later that day, a friend of my daughter's was looking at a photograph of the damaged car on her computer screen. As she looked at the image, her young son (aged four) spotted it and came over to her. "That's Charlotte's car," he stated. His mother was surprised. "How did you know?" she asked him. "Mike just told me," he said, gesturing to the side of him. "Look, there's Mike in the photograph, sitting on the top of the car!" His mother could see nothing, neither in the picture nor standing next to her son.

When the friend shared her story with my family, we were all blown away. Was "Mike," the young boy's invisible friend, the Archangel Michael or perhaps some other guardian spirit? Whoever he was, he certainly took care of my daughter and granddaughter that day. That wasn't the end of the story, though. The following day, my daughter posted another photograph of the wrecked car on the Internet and once again the young boy spotted the picture. He immediately pointed to the empty passenger seat of the car. "Look Mummy, Mike's sitting next to Charlotte in this picture." When his mother asked him where exactly, he became quite mad! It was clear enough to him, why couldn't his mother see? Are the bands of light inhabited by angels invisible to most humans? We know they are; but it's fabulous that some children can see them still.

Guardian Guidance

Take a camera or your camera phone and tour the old buildings in a big city or your local town. Photograph all the angels you can find. Look for them in churches and cathedrals, in churchyards, in parks—on fountains and statues, and on the outside of town halls and ancient buildings, carved into the stonework. Your local museum may have paintings you can snap or postcards you can buy. If you ask permission, you might find a few angels in your local gift store to photograph, too. Turn your images into a screensaver for your computer or background for your phone. That way your angels will always be close by.

SAVED BY AN ANGEL

Isn't the story of "Mike" and the little boy wonderful? Documenting personal angelic encounters like this make me know, without a shadow of a doubt, that angels are real ... of course they are! Have you had times in your life when you felt an angel intervened or kept you from danger? Write up what you remember in the appropriate section in Chapter 8.

A Few Facts about Angels

We still have so much to learn about the Guardian Angels in our lives, but here are a few things we can be sure about:

* Michaelmas is a day of angel celebration, known as the Feast of Saint Michael and All Angels. In the Western Christian church, this is celebrated on 29 September each year. The Greek Orthodox church honors the Archangels on 8 November. Traditionally, on Michaelmas Eve, nuts were cracked open in celebration, and during the day, a meal of goose was eaten along with a special cake, variously called struan Michael, Michaelmas bannock, and St Michael bread, in honor of the Archangel Michael and all angels.

* In the Bible, the Archangel Michael and the Archangel Gabriel are the only two angels mentioned by name.

* If you include fallen angels (who turned away from God), then two more are mentioned—Lucifer/Satan and Apollyon/Abaddon.

* Unlike humans, angels do not have free will. They are created to do the bidding of God and one of those assigned roles is to take care of humankind.

* Angels generally appear to humans in a clothed or cloaked form, wearing garments bathed in white or golden light.

* The theological study of angels is called angelology.

* In earlier times, infant mortality was far greater than it is today and the graves of babies filled many churchyards. The "cherubs" we recognize so well actually came about as a form of comfort for parents who had lost their children. They imagined that, in death, their babies would grow wings like angels in heaven, or even become angels.

* *There are around 273 references to angels in the Old and New Testaments.*
* *According to Wikipedia, a study conducted in 2002 included interviews with 350 people who had encountered angels. Like the people in the case histories in my books, these people experienced a variety of phenomena, including seeing angels, hearing them, sensing them, and even smelling a pleasant fragrance when they were around. Their experiences included warnings, and being literally lifted or pushed out of harm's way. The angels appeared to the people in the study in a variety of different ways, some as human-type figures with wings and others as radiant or beautiful human beings or beings of light.*
* *The first historical reference to angels is thought to be the carved angels created by the Sumerians (who lived in what is now Iraq, back in 3000 BCE).*

TIP

Look for angel-decorated items in secondhand and thrift stores. You might be able to build up your angelic library or even find gifts for friends. It's wonderful to help a charitable foundation at the same time as growing your collection.

"Standing over you are guardians, noble, recording, who know what you do."

Surat al-Infitar, 10-12, Qur'an

CHAPTER 2

Angels of Culture and History

The world over, and throughout history, angels have been a part of our lives on Earth. Whatever the era, they have formed part of our culture—take a look around you now, and you'll find references to angels in music, television, film, and books. Make them part of your home by collecting angel-inspired objects and creating an environment that will get you into an angelic frame of mind.

Angels of Television and Film

Angels are familiar to us from many television shows and movies. They are literally ingrained in our psyche. Television angels seem particularly popular. Perhaps even the sceptics like to believe there might be something else.

It's certainly comforting to know that we are not alone. Of course, there are way too many to include them all here, but I'd love to share a few of them with you. One of the most popular television shows of recent years is *Touched by an Angel*, a US drama starring Roma Downey as an angel and Della Reese as her angelic supervisor. The show premiered on CBS on September 21, 1994 and

ran for nine seasons. Although it finished in 2003, repeats are played all over the world right up to this day.

If you were around between 1984 and 1989, you may have caught the popular American show *Highway to Heaven*. Jonathan Smith, played by Michael Landon, is a probationary angel sent back to Earth to help people. If you missed this, don't worry. I spotted repeats in England very recently.

HERE ARE A FEW ANGEL MOVIES YOU MAY HAVE SEEN

Angels in the Outfield
Almost an Angel
The Bishop's Wife
City of Angels
Constantine
Ghost
Heart and Soul
Heaven can Wait
It happened One Christmas
It's a Wonderful Life
Jesus of Nazareth
Michael
Stairway to Heaven
The Preacher's Wife
Wholly Moses
Wings of Desire

MOVIE LIST

The list of movies is just a small selection. Have you seen any of these? Write a list of your favorites in the appropriate place in Chapter 8 and maybe add a few more you haven't seen but would like to. I think you'll enjoy collecting the names of others. Tick them off once you've viewed them.

Angels at Home

I love to decorate my home with angels—not real ones of course (although I can't be sure). These days you can buy household items decorated with all sorts of angel images.

Having angels in and around the place where you live can certainly bring them to mind several times a day, and it helps you to feel closer to your own Guardian Angel. Your home will have a sense of peace around it. People will notice and point it out as they step across your threshold. I always feel calm at home, as if having angel objects there attracts the angels themselves. Perhaps it does. Here are a few of the things I have in my house:

* ***Angel books*** *I have them stacked on shelves and tables. They're literally everywhere, but I love to incorporate them in my decorating scheme. Their covers are so pretty.*

* ***Angel cards*** *Divination and affirmation cards come in gorgeous boxes and look wonderful stacked on a shelf or table. I've even designed my own, and you could, too.*

* ***Angel figurines*** *I have a vast collection but am particularly fond of white or cream pottery figurines. Some of mine are sprayed gold (it's a decorating choice because I often pick up angel figurines at sales and in thrift stores and I'm not keen on the rainbow-colored or plastic ones). I also have carved wooden angels. Which angels would form your collection? Crystal carved angels are popular, too.*

* ***Angel windchimes and rainbow makers*** *I have window "clingers" in different colors, which filter light through my window. Chimes hang inside by the window and at my front door. I love to hear them as they clink together in a gentle breeze or when a door opens. You can also buy glass "cut" shapes that sit on a windowsill or attach directly to the glass. I've owned several of these angel-like shapes and they pick up the sunlight and spray rainbows around the room creating a magical "angelic" atmosphere.*

* ***Water feature*** *I have one of these in my conservatory, decorated with crystals and more angels. If you decide to have one, too, remember to keep the water topped up and clean it regularly to keep it fresh.*

I have angels sitting on dishes that are filled with crystals and mini angel cards, angel designs on pillows, glasses, clocks, vases, oil burners, bookends, and a kitchen apron, and angels clipped to plant sticks. Angels cling to my candles, decorate my candlesticks, and sit by my front door. I have an angel sitting on my birdbath and others hanging over the edges of shelves. Previously, I've owned mugs and even teapots with angels on them. If you love angels, the chances are you have angels in your life already. I usually have a few in my handbag, one on my keychain, angel "coins" in my purse, and angel "wallet cards," too.

I like to look for angel gift wrap and blank notecards decorated with angels, which double up as Christmas cards, birthday cards, and cards for pretty much every occasion! Angel tree-toppers can be adapted for everyday use and you'll find that plastic angel figurines can look a million dollars if you spray them with metallic paint. I love to hang them on cupboard door knobs or glue them onto mirrors. I like angel photo frames, too, and angels decorate my photo album and address book. It really is addictive. Those angels hide everywhere! Where are yours?

YOUR ANGEL ITEMS

Do you own angel-decorated items? You may have been attracted to them without even knowing. Walk around your home and take note. Where are your angels? Do you have them on clothing or jewelry? I even have angel soaps! I have a gorgeous glass carafe with a gold angel on the side and a matching drinking glass. My favorite item is a champagne bucket with a raised cherub figure on each side. It had been scratched in the store, so I bought it at a bargain price and sprayed it with a gorgeous gold-leaf-colored paint. Make a list of the angels you've purchased or angels that others have bought for you. Write it down in the appropriate place in Chapter 8.

Angel-inspired Objects

You don't need to spend lots of money (or any money) on collecting angel items. Decide on a theme before you start, so your collection doesn't look too messy, and make sure you have a safe place to store those items not displayed, away from inquisitive pets and children.

You can buy pretty boxes specifically, or decorate shoe boxes with angel gift wrap. I have a lovely collection of antique boxes, which are perfect for keeping my precious objects together. You might prefer to recycle gift boxes or keep objects safe in open dishes and bowls.

Around the Christmas holiday season, you'll find plenty of angel-decorated items—there is nothing prettier than an angel-themed tree. Then after Christmas, you'll probably find angel decorations are reduced in price, so don't forget to check. This is a wonderful time for angel fans to stock up on these precious items. You can always remove the more obvious seasonal attachments, such as holly, and spray-paint items to match your home, as I do. I like gold, but you can pick up any color from your local paint or craft store. Here are some other items you may like to include in your collection:

* *Angel cards As mentioned, I have a large collection of affirmation and divination cards with angel-inspired messages. If you want to save money, keep an eye out for used packs on sale at online bookstores, such as Amazon, or for any that may be given away with magazines. I have a few packs of those. Maybe someone will give you a set as a birthday or Christmas gift. Alternatively, why not have a go at making your own? You'll need a few pieces of craft card cut to equal size. On the blank side, write inspirational angelic sayings. Select one or two each day to motivate you.*

* *Angel boards Angel boards are used in a similar way to a Ouija board. The energy is much higher, though, and many people believe their spiritual guides and angels can communicate with them in this way. The boards have letters and numbers printed on them and some sort of pointer (planchette) is used with two or more persons touching it. The pointer will move around the board, spelling out your angelic messages. Each board*

comes with instructions, so you can decide for yourself if this is something that might interest you.

* **Angel pendulum** Pendulums have been used for many years by people wanting to find out information or locate lost or hidden items. A pendulum is actually any weight attached to a string or thread. In days gone by, women would attach their wedding ring to a piece of cotton and ask the question, "Am I pregnant?" or "Am I carrying a girl/boy?" The pendulum would swing backward and forward or up and down, or maybe rotate clockwise or anticlockwise. After doing a test check for yes or no, you can use the same technique to ask your angel questions. I have a lovely quartz crystal pendulum carved in the shape of an angel, but there are plenty to choose from.

* **Crystals** Lots of people collect crystals for their magical qualities and many are suitable for connecting to your Guardian Angel. They are inexpensive to buy and you can gather them in a bowl, carry them with you, or wear them as jewelry. The basic three are: Clear Quartz for giving power to your activities, Rose Quartz for unconditional love, Amethyst for magical or psychic energy. Other crystals you might enjoy include the Angel Wing Agate—its wing-like tube structure can help bring serenity into your life. I have several pieces of Angelite, a pretty blue and white crystal that is said to help with spiritual journeys (it may be worth holding if you enjoy meditations). Crystals come in all shapes and sizes and vary greatly in price. If you are attracted to crystals, why not start a collection of your own? Plenty of books are available to give you more information about them. Another way you can use crystals is to arrange them around your angel statues or carry a few small ones with you in a velvet pouch. Use your intuition when working with crystals. If stones other than the ones I've mentioned feel more angelic to you, go with your own thoughts and feelings. It's certainly fun anyway!

* **Angel books** Why not start a collection of your own? The more you learn about your Guardian Angel, the closer you will feel. I love to read about real-life angel experiences; doing so helps to remind me of similar

experiences of my own. You could designate a specific shelf or perhaps a basket where you might keep them all together.

* ***Incense and aromatherapy oils*** *Such a wide selection of lovely scents is available that it's easy to find something to your taste. When I'm writing or reading angel books, I love to burn some incense or infuse some aromatherapy oils into the room. It really helps to get me into the angelic frame of mind.*
* **Incense** *Suitable fragrances include natural flower scents and frankincense. Also look for Nag Champa, which is a natural incense with a wonderful healing scent, perfect for angelic work.*
   Oils *Use pure aromatherapy oils in order to benefit from the energy of the scent, rather than filling your home with chemical smells. Natural flower scents— especially rose, lavender, and rosemary—or vanilla work well. My favorite, and the most effective for angel work, is pure frankincense oil. Place a few drops into the water-well at the top of an oil burner, or look for a plug-in version wherever you buy your oils. Make sure you follow the instructions carefully, and never leave unattended.*

BOOK COLLECTION

Do you have any angel books already? Perhaps you have borrowed one or two from the library or received one as a gift from a friend. Make a note of your angel reading in Chapter 8 or make a note of books you'd like to add to your collection and tick them off once you have done so.

We are modern people with regular lives. We have shopping to do, kids to pick up from school, and housework that requires attention, but there is no reason why we can't fit in a little angel magic, too. Angels are part of our lives even if we don't acknowledge them, but it's more fun if we do.

Placing angel objects in our homes reminds us they are around. Asking them to help us or bring us signs makes their presence more noticeable, and recording these experiences helps us to summon up more of the same. The more you consciously connect to your own Guardian Angel, the more you become aware of her. Now let's look at some of the ways we can bring a little angel magic into our lives. We can be reminded of these beings of light all day long!

Angel Music

Have you noticed how many songs contain the word "angel"? For a long time, my phone ringtone was Robbie Williams' popular song '"Angels" so everyone knew it was my phone ringing! Older songs contain the phrase "angel dove," possibly because it rhymes with love!

Can you think of any songs that contain the word "angel"? There are way too many to list here (thousands probably) but you may have some favorites. Note the angel songs you love in the appropriate place in Chapter 8. I want my favorites playing at my funeral. They are my songs for life. Play them and people will think of me (I hope!).

Angel music is something entirely different. Years ago, after asking for a sign that my angels were with me, I heard the most wonderful choir-like vibrational tone. It felt like a thousand angels were singing in harmony, accompanied by harps or violins.

Since that time, I've had many folk share their own experiences with angel music. Those privileged to hear this unique sound feel lucky beyond belief.

Musicians who have heard the choir of the angels have tried to reproduce the music for themselves, and many others have also had a go (with varying success). I worked alongside the talented musician Llewellyn, describing to him the "journey" of the music I heard. Together we created the CD "Crystal Angels", which closely resembles what I heard that day. I love it.

Now I have a whole basket of CDs on my desk labelled "angel music" and produced by various artists. I find it wonderful to listen to (and absorb) as I write and go about my angelic work.

Other favorites include "Angel" by Patrick Hawes, "A Promise of Angels" by Midori, and "A Hundred Thousand Angels" by Bliss. If you want to work with angels, you may find angel music is a useful accompaniment to your angel kit. It really helps when you want to meditate with your angels and draw them closer.

ANGEL SONG

Have a look through your music collection. Gather together a playlist of angel-inspired music for times when you want to relax and draw your angels close. Make a list of any angel music you own and any you'd like to buy in Chapter 8. Tick off titles as you acquire them.

Angels Around the World

I wondered what sort of people believed in angels and where that belief might have come from. Angels of some sort—beings of light or guardians—appear in different religions around the world and have done so as far back as recorded history.

It is always difficult to get this right when a faith is not your own, but I have done my best here from my own understanding. These are general beliefs and, of course, cannot account for every individual concerned.

Islamic belief shows angels as beings of light, who were created before humans and eventually die. More angels are known and named than are referred to in the Bible, including Jibreel (Gabriel), the messenger, Mika'eel (Michael), Israfeel, and Malik. Many angels seem to be given specific tasks, including taking care of weather and being caretakers of humankind.

Angels are spiritual beings who serve God, according to Christian beliefs. The Bible shows how one of their earliest roles was praising God. The Bible also suggests that some angels are assigned specific tasks, including taking care of churches, nations, and individuals.

As a general system, Protestants and Catholics both believe in the existence of angels (following the principles of the Bible). The Catholic Bible includes apocryphal books not found in the Protestant Bible. One of these is the Book of Tobit, which mentions the Archangel Raphael (the healer angel), who is not

usually recognized by Protestants. Surprisingly, the term "Guardian Angel" is not actually mentioned in the Bible but is accepted by both Protestants and Catholics as an important part of the teaching.

The word "angel" is an ancient one. It is derived from the Greek word *angelos*, meaning messenger. *Malakh* is the Hebrew word for angel; it also means messenger. The Persian word for angel is *angaros*, which means a courier. Angel-like beings appear in many religions—avatars in Hinduism, devas and bodhisattvas in Buddhism, and the Greeks wrote about spirit beings they called daimons. In many ancient tribal civilizations, guardian spirits and guides are part of the ancient culture. For all the differences in beliefs around the world, one thing we all agree on is that angels are real.

Wings and Halos

Most of the people who write to me don't see angels with wings or halos.
They do sometimes describe a bright light surrounding the angel
in an egg shape. Yet for many hundreds of years, artists have
depicted angels with wings.

Early Christian artists added wings to their angels after being inspired by Greek art. Muslim artists were likely influenced by Persian illustrations. It has been suggested that Christian painters copied the idea of the heavenly halo (the light around the head of an angel) from the Greeks and Romans, who had already been using this idea for many years. The wings came about possibly because of the speed with which an angel would appear and disappear. Early peoples might have considered wings, like those of birds, to be the mostly likely form of transportation.

It seems that angels with wings and halos were added to religious artwork after receiving the approval of the Roman Council of Nicaea in AD 325. Today, our iconology mainly shows angels with a large set of white, feathery, bird-style wings, so we recognize them as different and distinct from human beings. I rather like angels being shown in this way and feel comforted by the idea of angel wings being used to hug and wrap around us to make us feel safe and loved.

When you imagine your own Guardian Angel, do you see wings and a halo in your mind's eye? If so, there is a high chance your angel will appear to you this way in dreams and visions so you won't feel afraid.

Guardian Guidance

Why not have a go at producing some angel art? It's a wonderful way of connecting to the energy of your own angel. You could draw your angel or something that simply feels like angel energy. If you're good at painting or drawing, try producing something from scratch. Create something modern, or be inspired by ancient artists from history. If you need a little more support, use the phrase "free angel coloring" to search the internet and find outlines of

Angels love us

Many of my readers write to tell me about the relationship they have with their own Guardian Angel. People experience angels in different ways, but they all feel the unconditional love they bring. I thought this experience was beautiful.

"I feel they teach and guide me, tell me what to do and where to go. They've helped and protected me all my life. I even sense them speak to me. When I see them, the room can be full of them and I know every one of them—but not as relations; it's as if I have been with them. They tell me to trust them and they tell me they love me and will look after me.

I've seen them for years but still doubt myself. I think they teach me because there are things I need to know, which I knew before in the spirit world and have forgotten on Earth. I know it sounds crazy (sometimes even to me) but I always feel so much love from them all."

Sandra

angel images. You can print out the ones you like and color them in. Your local craft store may sell angel-inspired products you could incorporate into your art. You can trace them and paint in the outlines, so that the result mimics stained-glass windows; or cut out the white areas and stick in fine, colored tissue papers in place of glass. (I remember doing this at school and sticking the images on the classroom windows so the light would shine through the colored tissue.) Alternatively, work with felt-tipped pens, glitter, or stick-on felt, with shiny paper or real feathers for wings. Use good-quality paper and then you can frame your work afterward.

CHAPTER 3

Angels of Healing, Guidance, and Protection

Your Guardian Angel is never far away—there to heal you in times of pain, guide you to make the right decisions, comfort you in times of sadness, and even help you to handle everyday stresses. When back-up is needed, they may call on the more powerful Archangels for greater strength, support, and specific help and healing.

An Angel by Your Side

Our Guardian Angel is always with us, every day. Our angels are in the background, watching over our choices. They don't spy on us but draw closer and pull away as required.

If you think of them, they know. If you need them, they feel this, too. They quietly wait and watch to see how they might be needed, but if you call upon them, they're on full alert. No—they don't watch you in the bath (I get asked that a lot!).

If you need them to intervene, its okay to ask them—in fact, you should. Angels know how important it is that we live our lives and make our own choices, so generally they'll stay back unless we ask them for help.

"An angel can illuminate the thought and mind of man by strengthening the power of vision."

St. Thomas Aquinas (priest, philosopher, and theologian)

Here are a few of the ways in which your angel might support you:

* *A little courage goes a long way. Your Guardian Angel might be able to bring you an extra boost of energy before you give a speech at work or before an interview or legal meeting—any occasion when you're going to feel wobbly. Then you'll know that, as the event goes ahead, you'll perform at your very best. You'll feel great afterward, knowing you accomplished your task and you had a little sneaky support.*
* *Angels are well known for appearing at times when we need a little healing support. Many people write to tell me that they saw their Guardian Angel the first time when they were in hospital or when their body was in crisis following an accident. Your angel might appear at the end of the bed or in the doorway, or she may just whisper encouraging words of support.*

* *Occasionally, people see their angels as their soul lifts from the body during a near-death experience or while in deep meditation. The experience doesn't automatically mean you're going to die, so don't panic. Your angel's role is usually to calm you and then send you back to your body again. Your angel may sit with you while doctors operate on your body or stay with you when your body is temporarily unconscious or in a very relaxed state. It's a great opportunity to just hang out together and might be the only time you see your Guardian Angel face to face.*

* *Guardian Angels have been known to take away pain and even physical symptoms of illness.*

* *Some people joke about how they ask angels to find them parking spaces but there is some validity in this. There is no need to worry about asking your Guardian Angel to do something you feel might be too trivial for her. Angels seem to enjoy helping us with simple tasks. I think it helps us to feel connected to them more, and they help when they can. For example, maybe they could lead you to an elusive ingredient you need for a recipe, or help you to get to an important meeting in time by ensuring the traffic lights are on your side.*

* *Angels can sometimes recover lost objects and it's certainly worth asking them to give it a go.*

TIP

Wear a piece of angel jewelry or carry an angel coin or card with you wherever you go. It will make you feel closer to your Guardian Angel. You can find all these and more at gift and greetings card stores or search on the Internet for other inspirational gifts.

Angels help with missing ring

"*Thirty years ago, when my gran was ill, I used to take care of her. One day she took off her wedding ring and placed it on my finger. It was such a wonderful gift and she told me it was a token of her love.*

Sadly, not long after this, she became too ill for me to look after and she moved to a care home. It wasn't long before dementia took away her memories and she didn't remember any of us. It hurt so much.

Last year, I lost some weight and with it my gran's ring. I was devastated and looked everywhere. In the end, I decided to ask my Guardian Angel to help me, and then I forgot about it. Sometime later, I was sitting reading a book when I noticed the sun shining through the window. Nestled in the fibers of the rug, glistening in the beam of light, was Gran's ring! I totally believe the angels helped me to recover this precious memento; there seems no other explanation. The rug had been vacuumed several times since I'd lost the ring. Whatever happened that day, I'm so grateful to have the ring back safely in my possession."

Lesley

What is the Role of a Guardian Angel?

The traditional role of angels is as protectors and guides and their role is really very similar today.

There have always been stories about angels helping people but, unlike today, when we can look up angels on the Internet and read about them in books, it may have been harder to find something relevant to everyday life in days gone by.

We can judge their roles today by reading of other people's angel experiences and the stories seem to fall into various categories:

* *Angels guide us to meet the people who can help us or set us on the right path.*
* *They lift us physically out of danger or get a stranger (an angel in disguise?) to distract us so that we avoid an unexpected hazard.*
* *They bring people (angels again?) to speak to us and comfort us. Stories persist of strangers stopping to share helpful words and guidance at appropriate times.*
* *They bring useful people to us when we're in trouble. I've collected numerous stories about people being helped by random folk who seem to have the perfect equipment to fix their car on the deserted country road or offer food, money, or shelter unexpectedly. These people often disappear as quickly as they arrived, usually before they can be thanked.*
* *A confident "person" protects us from a threatening individual either by appearing bigger and more powerful or by just barring the way from the menace.*
* *Angels leave us signs to guide us to our next step (see Chapter 4).*

* *They comfort us by bringing sounds, scents, lights, or even physical objects, or by surrounding us with a loving, peaceful energy or touch.*
* *They may escort deceased loved ones to us (in visions and dreams) to reassure us, or bring through the voice of a deceased family member whose warning may startle us to action more quickly—STOP, SLOW DOWN, for example.*

Comfort and protection seem key to the tasks of our Guardian Angels, but they can also guide us, offering us light on the path ahead or perhaps leading us to one trail rather than another. Some roads may be rocky and fraught with danger, whereas others might be safer and full of more interesting or helpful experiences, and it is not always clear which way is best. Our angels can suggest ideas or highlight certain paths, although in every case the choice is ultimately ours.

Angels can't tell us what to do but might step in if we are way off track in our lives. If we get in with the wrong crowd or get involved with criminal activities, they might find ways of steering us away. However, it might be in our best interests to suffer the consequences of our actions, so they often stand back when you'd think they'd step in.

They can't solve every problem or fix every wrong; nor would we want them to. Part of our mission on Earth as human souls is to learn, for our spirits to grow from experience. More growth can often come about from working out what went wrong or learning how to handle a crisis.

Of course, when you're frightened, in peril, sad, or lost, your angel can help. One of the most important things for us to learn when connecting to our angels is that angels can intervene but not interfere. For them to get involved we need to give them permission—even a straightforward "HELP!" counts. My experience shows that some of the most dramatic of all angelic interventions occur after one shouts for help!

You don't need to use magical words or memorize a particular phrase. I like to make a request in the same way I might speak to a dear friend. Indeed, angels are our dearest friends. They know us,

understand us, and accept us exactly as we are. That means always beginning a request with the word "please" and ending with the words "thank you." You could explain a little about the problem and how you'd like them to intervene, but by using words such as, "I give you permission to find the best way to solve the problem," you leave a little leeway for magic to occur.

We can't always see the whole plan or understand that something is happening in the way that it is for a good reason. Angels might have a better overview, and if by falling and twisting your ankle it means your future husband (currently a stranger to you) has the opportunity to rescue you, you might not be so keen to stop the flow of events. Some of life's more annoying incidents have been set up so that we can learn a great lesson. These new coping strategies could be important in the future and angels know this. Let them help you to solve the problem or support you as you live through them. Asking for this aid (as often as you like) is the answer.

TIP
Why not have an angel-inspired get-together with friends?
You could read out some of the stories from this book
and each of you could chat about your beliefs
and experiences.

Angels of healing

I know some people struggle with the idea that angels can help with healing, but I've experienced the phenomenon myself. I've written about it before, but if you missed it, here is what happened to me.

Years ago I was just reaching the end of a long train journey, sitting in a separate carriage with no one else in sight. I had a raging toothache and no painkillers on me. In agony I called out to my Guardian Angel to help me. "Please take away my pain until I can get to a dentist tomorrow," I asked out loud. I lay back with my eyes closed and suddenly began to relax. Within no time at all, the pain began to subside and I felt so much better. I have no other explanation but that my Guardian Angel stepped in to help. I still went to the emergency dentist the following day for treatment but managed to get a good night's sleep in the meantime.

I regularly ask the angels to take away my fear when I sit in the dentist's chair or have to go for a hospital appointment. Sometimes the fear of pain is the worst part of all. Why not give this a go next time you have a medical appointment? Angels are not doctors and we still need professional care, but there's no harm in pulling in a little back-up, now is there?

Recently, I was suffering from various health problems, picked up by a blood test, one of which was high cholesterol. One night I woke to see a group of beings around my bed. I couldn't see them clearly but they became aware of the fact that I had awoken. A voice reassured me, "Don't worry, Jacky, we're healing you. Go back to sleep!" I could see a figure with long blonde hair floating toward my bedroom door!

The memory was clear to me the following day and, if I'm honest, it was a little spooky. Then I had another blood test and a couple of days later called the doctor's for my results. The receptionist said pleasantly, "Yes, everything is okay. It says, 'No more action needed.'" I was so stunned, I rang back to double check. "Sorry, did you say that my test results were all okay now?" She had!

Guardian Guidance

When you feel anxious or stressed, try to find a quiet place to sit or lie down for a few moments. Imagine a whole host of angels surrounding you and directing beams of healing light down into your body through their open-palmed hands. Imagine the energy massaging your aura—the electrical energy field that surrounds your physical body. In your mind's eye, see your angels as they use these beams of light to calm and relax you. Enjoy the sensation for a few minutes, or even for half an hour or so if you have time. Absorb the peaceful feeling and just relax.

When you're finished, sit up slowly and bring your mind back into the everyday world. You may feel as though you've just woken from a refreshing sleep. Have a warm drink to ground yourself and come back slowly into the present moment. Enjoy!

TIP
If you're waiting for emergency treatment, for yourself or others, ask the angels to draw close and help. Many people feel instantly calm, knowing they are not alone.

Healed by my angel

"Several years ago I had a nasty chest infection. I was very sick and on a lot of medication—three types of inhaler, steroids, antibiotics. The illness went on for over three months and the doctor said it was prolonged by my stressful job, young children, and the fact that my husband worked opposite shifts to me.

One night, my husband went to bed in our attic bedroom and I was downstairs. Scarily, I had a severe asthma attack and I started to panic. I couldn't get my inhalers to work and found I was not getting enough air into my lungs. I tried to call my husband but he couldn't hear me, and in my panic, it didn't occur to me to phone for an ambulance.

Terrified, I called out for help in my head and asked my angels to assist me. It was then that I heard a voice say, 'Lie down,' so I immediately lay down on the sofa. I closed my eyes and through my closed lids saw flashes of brilliant blue lights around me, like fireworks. Almost at once my breathing returned to normal, yet I'd taken no medication and not used my inhalers.

Shortly after that terrifying episode I was given the opportunity to leave my stressful job and go back to my old job where I was welcomed with open arms. My illness cleared up and I didn't need my inhalers after that. I am so grateful to the angels for so much more than that instant healing they gave me. They also helped me to move on to a much better and happier phase of my life."

Maureen

Archangels to Guide You

As we've already seen, our Guardian Angels like to steer us through life's challenging pathways, but other angels can help with these tasks, too.

Various ancient books contain lists of angels who are higher and more powerful than the Guardian Angels. These are the Archangels—"Arch" means "chief"—and we've already mentioned a few. Archangel names and numbers vary from religion to religion; some say there are seven others twelve or more. Here are the most frequently quoted Archangels, each of whom has been assigned different tasks by God. If you need a powerful intervention and want to request that a specific Archangel help you, use the list below to guide you. You can call upon the Archangels in the same way that you'd ask your Guardian Angel to help you.

You don't need to remember the names or roles of the Archangels if you don't want to. Be guided by your Guardian Angel, and just ask if you feel that stronger energy is required. In any case, rest assured your Guardian Angel will bring in the back-up team if it's needed, even if you forget to ask. Alternatively, imagine that the angel with the most relevant experience is by your side. Visualize clearly and know it is done.

"Be guided by your Guardian Angel, and just ask if you feel that stronger energy is required."

Archangel and name meaning	How they can help you
Ariel Lion of God	Ariel can help with anything that is connected to nature and the animal kingdom, including birds and fish. Many believe that Ariel is in charge of the very spark of nature watched over by the "faerie" realms, including all trees, plants, and flowers.
Azrael Whom God helps	Azrael helps to escort our loved ones to the afterlife. He is also the earthly record keeper. Call upon this angel when loved ones are close to passing on, or to help gather information for a family tree or organize photographs, for example.
Chamuel He who sees God	An Archangel with a massive role—the seemingly impossible task of keeping peace in the world. He can help with smaller disputes and legal battles and has been known to step in to retrieve lost items.
Gabriel God is my strength	The angel most known as a messenger and so helpful in all activities involving communication—letters, e-mails, telephone calls, or getting your message across correctly.
Haniel Grace of God	An angel for women, Haniel is strongly associated with the moon and moon cycles. He can help with all of your mystical or spiritual endeavors, and with rituals that involve working with crystals, lotions, and potions! Love it!

Archangel and name meaning	How they can help you
Jophiel Beauty of God	For anything to do with craft or creativity, call upon this Archangel. Jophiel is useful for manifesting and making things, taking an idea from paper or in your head and turning it into reality.
Metatron Angel of the presence	Metatron is connected with jobs, marriage, family, and children. You can call upon his assistance with all of your relationships.
Michael He who is like God	Michael is the protection angel, perfect to call upon when you need to be brave and long for a sidekick to give you confidence.
Raphael God heals	Raphael has been adopted by many hospitals and healing institutions. If you need support during medical procedures, or even assistance if you work in the healing profession, call upon this Archangel.
Sandalphon Prince of prayers	This Archangel is a prayer carrier. He lifts your prayers up to God. You can call upon him for all spiritual advice and support.
Uriel Light of God	Uriel works with all the bigger aspects of earthly life and is concerned with the healing of the planet after major natural phenomena, such as floods, fires, and earthquakes. Send Uriel to all the troubled areas around the world.

Michael

Does this story feature an angel in disguise? Perhaps we'll never understand the exact purpose of this interaction but it certainly has a sense of mystery about it.

"Back in 2012, my husband and I were out together on a three-hour road trip. About an hour after leaving home we passed a hitchhiker. Neither my husband nor I pick up hitchhikers normally, but when we passed this one I had this unsettling feeling that we needed to turn around and pick him up. The feeling was so strong that I turned to my husband. "Babe …" was all I'd said, when he replied, "We need to turn around?" We both felt we had to help the man.

When I spoke to the man, I actually gasped. He looked right at me with the purest white eyes! I didn't say anything to my husband because I thought my own eyes must be playing tricks on me! We were driving our truck that day (which was a last-minute decision) so the only place for the man to ride was in the back of the truck. It was still cold, being early spring, so my husband gave him a jacket to help keep him warm. I will admit I was a little wary, with all the horrific things you hear about, and I kept watching him through the window, hoping he didn't have a gun in his backpack.

An hour and a half later we pulled into a gas station and my husband and I went in to get "our friend" something to eat and drink. He looked up and this

time his eyes were the most piercing blue I'd ever seen! After leaving the gas station to continue our journey, I finally decided to ask my husband if he'd noticed anything about the hitchhiker's eyes. He hesitated before saying white then blue. We'd both seen the strange phenomenon.

We reached our final truck stop about 45 minute later and told our passenger we'd be glad to get him a bus ticket to help him get to where he needed to go. He politely declined and stated firmly that he never took public transportation. He and my husband went inside to use the restroom and I said a little prayer, asking for a sign that we'd done the right thing. I suggested inwardly to my angels that if our passenger was called Jesus or Michael I would know for sure.

I stopped by the ATM and withdrew some cash to help him on his journey. By this time he and my husband were outside chatting together and as I approached him I held out my hand to give him the cash. He humbly accepted the money and reached out to shake my hand and introduce himself. I was blown away when he told me his name … it was Michael! I think my jaw pretty well hit the ground.

My husband and I got back into our truck and as we turned around to wave goodbye … he was nowhere to be found! We looked everywhere, but he'd totally disappeared!"

Tammy

Guardian Guidance

Affirmations are words and phrases you can use to condition your mind. They can be especially useful if you want to connect to your Guardian Angel. By repeating the phrase over and over again, you can become more open to the suggestion it contains. If you wish, you could write down your affirmation and put it somewhere to remind you of it. You could read it every morning as you get dressed or perhaps recite it out loud just before you brush your teeth. Getting into a routine is the best way to remember to use your affirmation. If you prefer, you could work with more than one at once, or move on to a new one after a few weeks.

You can make up your own affirmations or select from one of the following.

I am open to communication from my angels.

I am happy for my Guardian Angel to rescue me in times of need.

My angel keeps me calm in challenging situations.

I am aware at all times and notice signs that my angel is with me.

Your affirmations can be about you connecting to your angel or asking your angel to support your activities. Why not give it a go?

Angels of Protection

According to many sources, protection is one of the angels' most important roles. Let's have a look at a few ways in which they have helped people in the past.

* *When people have felt frightened and asked for angelic assistance, they have instantly felt calmed and more in control, which has helped them to make clear-headed, sensible decisions to get themselves out of a scary situation.*

* *Several people have told me how they felt someone tug on their coat, literally lifting them out of danger of a speeding vehicle. When they spun around to thank their guardian, no one was there.*

* *Angels often draw close when we travel. They like to sit with us when we drive or accompany us on the back of our bicycles. Many people have written to me to tell me about life-saving situations they experienced after hearing a voice.*

* *Some people have experienced a strange urging that made them take a different route to work, or not go out at all that day. It's only afterward that they realized this may have helped them to avoid an accident or stopped them getting killed. (I'll be honest and say I wish I totally understood why everyone isn't saved every time.)*

I've had experiences like the following one numerous times. Recently, I took my mother and her neighbor to visit a family friend, Graham, in a local nursing home. I'd been several times to visit but this time I had an overwhelming gut feeling that I should take his friends, too, as if this would be our last opportunity. When we arrived at the nursing home, Graham was in great spirits and the staff brought us all a cup of tea. We had a real party, chatting about old times, and I promised I would bring the two ladies to visit again. Yet in my heart I knew this was the final time.

The following week, I was able to borrow the car again, unexpectedly, and so arranged another visit. Unknown to us, our friend had fallen into a coma and was now close to death. We were able to hold his hand and kiss him goodbye but, of course, he was unconscious, so we could only hope he knew we were there. I was so grateful for the psychic urging I'd had the week before. It was the one day when everyone was well enough for the visit and everything came together perfectly. I silently thanked my Guardian Angel for helping us to take advantage of that last opportunity.

If you get a strong feeling like this, there is a high chance your Guardian Angel is reaching out to you. Here are a couple more real-life situations:

* *When faced by a gang of vicious thugs, a woman ran from the leader, who chased her down an alleyway. As the man approached her, she seemed to have become invisible to him and the confused man turned and walked away.*
* *One young girl heard a voice in her head yell at her to run away as a man approached her on her way home from school. She gave her parents a description of the man and they called the police. He was caught and it turned out the police were already looking for him. He'd already hurt someone else in the area a few days earlier.*

If you're worried about your travels, why not make a point of asking your angels to stay close by. You can even ask your angels to help friends and relatives. You might like to reinforce your request by putting a bumper sticker on your car or wearing an angel pin bearing the words: "Protected By Angels." It certainly can't hurt, anyway.

> "Angels often draw close when we travel. They like to sit with us when we drive or accompany us on the back of our bicycles."

CHAPTER 4

Signs that your Guardian Angel is Around

My books are full of the real-life stories of ordinary folk who have had one-off experiences of angelic intervention. Angels step in during times of need and people might feel an invisible hand resting upon theirs or perhaps a reassuring touch upon the shoulder. Discover these and the other signs that your Guardian Angel is ever present.

Subtle Signs

Rarely, people might hear a voice calling their name or warning them of danger, but many more feel guided by an inner or gut instinct, or feel a sense of reassurance and peace after asking for angelic support.

If you're really lucky, your angel may begin to reach out to you on a regular basis. It's important that angels don't frighten us and initially their approach may be very subtle. As any incident occurs, we need to assimilate that information and get used to the idea that something paranormal or occult, that is something unknown or beyond normal, has happened to us. Once we've accepted and got used to the idea, often more contact occurs.

Guardian Angels don't all work in the same way. They seem to adapt their approach according to their personality or ours. Some angels are more hands-on than others. They like to make it clear that they are with us. Some are gentle and prefer to stand back and wait to be invited in.

Most angels use signs to show that they are with us. It's hard for them to manifest fully into our dimension. Their world is so different from ours. Our human eyes find it almost impossible to see them, so they use other tricks! Here are some of them:

* *A white feather In your time of need, your Guardian Angel may bring a white feather as a gift to let you know that she is around. The white feather is a classic sign, which says, "We are here for you, we are supporting you; you are not alone." You'll probably find your white feather in an unexpected place, or it will appear in a place where no feather existed just moments before. A feather is a safe and gentle way for your angels to show you they are with you. This is one of the most common of all the angel signs and I'm sure you've heard of it. White feathers are known as the calling card of the angels and they can be any size. Some people find lots of little white fluffy feathers and others find larger swan-sized quills. Have you ever found feathers of your own? Their appearance can be quite unexpected or they might appear in an unusual way.*

* **Angel music** It's rare but if you're very lucky, you may hear the sound of the celestial choir, as I did. Angel music sounds as if a million angels are singing in harmony, accompanied by an orchestra of harps. I guess it sounds exactly the way you feel it ought to sound! Musicians have tried many times to reproduce angel music of their own and their tracks do sound similar, although without the vibration of the angels you will never get an exact replica. The angelic choir is said to be praising God, the Creator Being, and is one of the most memorable ways in which angels can communicate with us.

* **Small gifts** Some angels leave small coins (pennies from heaven), crystals, or pebbles as presents. These seemingly insignificant tokens can mean a lot if you are looking for a keepsake. It can be nice to own something tangible that you can keep in a special place as a reminder that your Guardian Angel is a real being.

* **Media signs** After asking your angel for help, your sign might come in a surprising way. You might be flicking through a book or magazine and come across an article or paragraph that contains the information you are seeking. You could change the television channel and a news reporter will be discussing the very thing you are interested in, or perhaps you overhear a conversation between strangers. Be alert after asking for help—your angels will guide the information to you.

* **Coincidences** What a fun way for angels to reach out to us! We all experience coincidences from time to time, those moments when unexpected things come together in the perfect way. Perhaps you have asked your angel for help in obtaining a particular item. A friend who happens to pop by is, coincidently, looking for a new home for the very item you want.

   Another scenario is that you might bump into an old friend several times after not seeing her for years. Maybe the two of you

need to chat to discover why. It could be that your angel is setting something up. Know that coincidences are just another way of your angel bringing you a sign.

* **Scents** *When angels are around, many people notice an accompanying fragrance. The most common is the smell of flowers, especially roses. If you are with other people, an extraordinary phenomenon may occur. Half of those present may notice the overwhelming smell while the other half notice nothing at all. The smell will suddenly fill the air and then disappear without warning, as quickly as it arrived. Other common scents include vanilla and a recognizable odor of perfume or aftershave. This means that the angel is accompanying a deceased loved one. The scent is a beautiful reminder of a loving human soul. Feel honored by this gift. If you suddenly smell the overpowering scent of a bouquet of flowers, it*

could be that your angel is standing close by. They love to arrive on a drift of flower scents.

* ***Touch*** *Angels do physically touch people, but it's usually quite subtle. However, there is no mistaking that comforting (and invisible) hand upon your shoulder or an angelic hand clasping yours. You may feel a tingling sensation or a sense of being away from the pain or fear for a moment or*

Angel on a bus

Angels love to bring us signs that they are around and they often appear in the most unusual of ways.

"On Sunday afternoon, I was on the way home with my son, after visiting friends. We were sitting on the bus and I was thinking about my Guardian Angel. I looked up at the sky, and as I did so, I asked my angel to bring me a sign that she was with me. Just then I glanced through the window and at that exact moment, a bus passed us going in the opposite direction. I was stunned when I realized that the bus had an advertisement on the side, part of which read ANGEL. I'd had my sign!"

Lucia

two. The air around you may change or time may seem to stand still while the experience takes place.

* **Technology** Angels are quite capable of switching your television channel for a good reason or arranging for you to notice a special tune on the radio. I once had a television come on when it wasn't plugged in! Be alert to contact via answering machines, mobile phones, text messages, and so on. Angels are ingenious and great at manipulating electronics in our modern world!

* **Shapes and forms** Some people see angels, or wings, in all sorts of everyday situations. You might notice a beautiful feather shape streaking across a cloudy sky, or the flame on your candle flicker and create the striking shape of angel wings. People see angels in bubbles, food, and many other things. Perhaps your angel sign will appear in this way. Watch out for rainbows as signs or a sudden beam of light illuminating something important.

TIP

Why not ask your own angels to appear in a dream. If you ask them each night before you fall asleep, you'll increase your chances of seeing them.

CONNECTING WITH YOUR ANGELS

How would you like your Guardian Angel to let you know that she is with you? You do have some say in the matter. What would make you feel more comfortable? Would you prefer your angels to reach out to you with white feathers, or maybe you'd rather perform angelic rituals and have them draw close to you then? Some people see angels when they meditate and you could ask your own angels to contact you when you're in this more relaxed state of mind. Have a think about it and then make a note of your thoughts in the angel journal section in Chapter 8. Your angels will certainly take note of your preference and try to comply as best as they can.

* ***Sleep contact*** *Many of my own angel experiences occur when I'm fast asleep. My body may be resting but my mind is totally aware of what is happening. My angels appear during this time because this is when I find it easier to work through problems with them. They don't usually look like angels when I see them, though. Often it's only when I awake that I realize I've been communing with the angels!*

Feathers from heaven

"My mother, sister, and I have always believed in angels and like to keep an eye out for feather signs. Mom said that if anything ever happened to her, she would try to reach out to make contact with her girls.

Sometime later, when Mom was seriously ill, I was sitting by her bedside, talking to Dad about how angels were always around to help. As we talked, I noticed something by Mom's head—three white feathers, one for each of us! The hospital didn't use feather pillows so we knew it was an angel sign. The feathers brought us all great comfort when we needed it the most."

Amy

Feather surprise

This story is typical of the lovely experiences readers have.
"I started to read your books last year on vacation and was interested
in the sections about white feathers. My friend and I chatted
about it and I asked her if she thought I'd have anyone '
up there' looking after me.

I've never found any feathers or anything like that but later I
had a big surprise. That night I went shopping and when I opened
my purse to buy something, I found a white feather nestled inside.
I couldn't believe it!"

Laura-Jayne

Guardian Guidance

Why not collect the angel feathers that you find when you ask for a sign. Here are a few things you could do with them.

* *Pop them into get-well cards or attach to gifts so that you send a little angel energy along with your love.*
* *Collect them in a pretty jar or pot.*
* *Glue them to angel statues and figurines for customized decorations.*
* *Carry a few in your purse and hand them to friends who seem upset or worried.*
* *Gather them in a drawstring bag and place them under your pillow.*

Angel Feather Colors

White feathers are the ones that most people find. Occasionally, I hear stories of other feather colors and these variations do seem to have slightly different meanings. I've studied numerous feather stories and here are my suggestions. Have you found feathers of other colors?

* **White** *This common angel gift means, "I am around you, everything will be okay, don't worry."*
* **Black** *Black feathers tend to appear in times of crisis or stress, or at least when we are going through a challenging period. One of these seems to indicate, "I am aware of your difficulties and I'm here to support you while you work your way through them."*
* **Yellow** *Such an uplifting sign, a yellow feather seems to say, "Well done! Everything is working well for you in your life at the moment. We are with you to celebrate your success."*
* **Pink** *Your angels are enjoying the fun and laughter or joining in with the big joke. It's a real light-hearted sign and full of joy. Your angels are engaging with you in a wonderful way and sharing your pleasure, not laughing at the situation.*
* **Blue** *This is the sign of peace. A blue feather may be an indication that you should rest more, find more time to relax and slow down. Your angel is supporting your choices to find harmony in your life.*
* **Red** *Red is commonly used for love, romance, and even passion. If you need these energies boosting in your life, a red feather may be a welcome sign.*
* **Green** *A green feather often indicates that healing is being given. Accept this feather with grace at this wonderful blessing, and look for more healing opportunities in your life.*
* **Gray** *Not quite white and not quite black, a gray feather shows your angel is close by, keeping an eye on the current situation. Stay hopeful as your angel is helping in every way possible.*

Guardian Guidance

Just for fun, how about making your own feather chart? You can easily buy colored feathers from craft suppliers if necessary. I found many colored feathers blowing about at a local bird sanctuary! Using a piece of card, stick down your colored feathers and write out your own explanations next to them. Use mine, if you like, or if you've received different colored feathers in the past, you may be able to fine-tune the meanings for your own chart.

"I saw the angel in the marble and

carved until I set him free."

Michelangelo (sculptor, painter, and architect)

Guardian Guidance

If you enjoy collecting angel feathers, you might like to save them in a book, along with a record of all of your other angel signs. Make a note of when and where you found them, why you feel they appeared when they did—maybe you asked for the experience—and what they mean to you. By acknowledging the signs you receive in this way, you are saying, "Thank you. I received your message and look forward to more," and it will help to imprint your experiences on your mind, serving as a reminder of how many times your angels have helped and guided you. You'll find it easier to recognize more signs once you acknowledge the ones you've had. Leave space to write a follow-up note to record what happened afterward. You'll grow closer to your Guardian Angel as you learn how to communicate with each other.

CHAPTER 5

Angel Meditations and Exercises

To reach out to your Guardian Angel using meditations is simple. As a young girl, I was bemused by meditation. I couldn't understand why thousands and thousands of people around the world would sit for hours with their eyes closed. I simply didn't "get" it. What on earth could they be doing? I just didn't see the point of it, but of course, I had no idea what I was missing. Let me share some wonderful meditations and exercises with you; they are designed to bring you closer to your Guardian Angel.

What is Meditation?

As a spiritual practice, meditation, or silent contemplation, has been used for thousands of years. The aim is to close down our outer world so that we can listen to our inner world, or our inner voice. Sit in a quiet space and get rid of day-to-day chatter by concentrating on a single thought or idea, or you could completely clear your mind.

There are other types of meditation, too. Some involve special breathing exercises; some are used for relaxation purposes. Meditation can help you to become less stressed or enable you to reach into the deeper parts of the mind. Some people who practice meditation regularly, and for prolonged periods, have profound paranormal or psychic experiences, including out-of-body travel, also known as astral projection, when the spirit lifts from the body; meeting angels and guides; seeing and experiencing extraordinary colors, signs, and symbols; and even encountering different realms. If you want to become more psychic, meditation is a great place to start.

Without too much difficulty, you can do a simple relaxation exercise, which can lead you to guided meditation, that is a voice-guided mental journey. On that journey, you can learn to connect with your Guardian Angel on a regular basis. Many different meditation techniques are open to you to try. Some people spend many years developing their technique, but let's try a few simple ideas to get you started.

TIP

Find a quiet place where you won't be disturbed. Make sure that you're warm enough to concentrate. Your body temperature often drops a little during meditation, so have a blanket nearby or turn up the heating slightly ... or wear socks!

Getting Started

Your first attempts at meditation might just be sitting quietly with your eyes closed while your mind relaxes or concentrates on a single word, phrase, or object (such as a candle flame). Have you ever tried to meditate but found yourself too distracted and so gave up? That happens to most people. Here are a few ideas to help:

* *Switch off the phone, take the dog to the neighbors, and stick a note on the door saying, "DO NOT DISTURB."*
* *Play relaxing music—new-age style music, especially angel music, is good.*
* *Have some natural background noises, such as birdsong or the ocean. Try your local new-age store or garden center for these.*
* *How about meditating to the background of an indoor waterfall? The calming sound will soothe you and help you to relax.*
* *Light a scented votive—place it in a glass holder and make sure it is well away from the drapes!—to help you drift away.*
* *Burn some incense.*

MEDITATION NOTES

What did you experience during this first practice? Do it two or three times until you are familiar with what to do and comfortable with doing it. Write down what you experienced in the appropriate section of Chapter 8 and add to your notes each time you do it, especially if there are any variations.

Guardian Guidance

First, find a small angel figurine, or a round-edged crystal if you don't have an angel. Then sit in a comfortable chair—a high-backed chair is ideal—and place your feet flat on the floor, or on a pillow if your feet don't reach the floor. Examine your angel or crystal closely. Admire the shape and colors.

Next, close your eyes. Feel and appreciate the shape of the object in your hands. Just let your mind drift toward the energy of the angel, or into the center of the crystal. "Feel" the colors, feel the energy, and do this with your mind. Hold that thought, and do not let your mind drift to anything else. When you are ready, open your eyes and bring yourself back into the room.

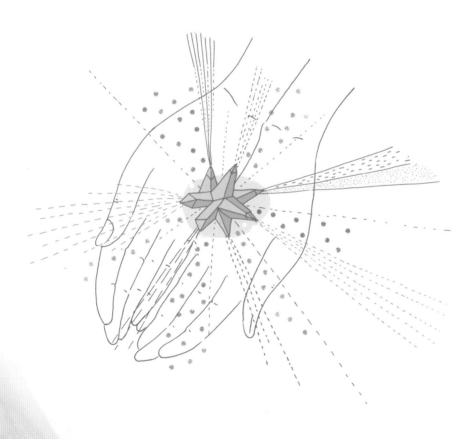

A Guided Meditation

This entails being taken on a mental journey either by following a talking meditation on CD or having someone read out the words for you. Alternatively, you could record your own script and play it back.

Guided meditations are useful for people who find it hard to quieten their mind, or are easily disturbed by outside distractions. Those people who like to do something or go somewhere in their mind may find that this type of meditation works best for them. Many new-age stores sell guided-meditation CDs, or try the Internet for a wider variety. I've produced several myself.

To get into a deeper state of trance, it's helpful to relax your body first of all. Pre-recorded CDs will have included this. The exercise may involve relaxing each part of the body in turn, imagining walking along the seashore, floating in a hot-air balloon, or walking up or down steps. All the while, with each action, the voice recording will encourage you to become more and more relaxed. In this next exercise I have used the idea of waves rushing in and receding to help you to relax. Take your time to savor each step. You could play a sea-sounds track in the background or even do the exercise on a beach. Give it a go.

"Guided meditations are useful for people who find it hard to quieten their mind."

Guardian Guidance

1 *Take a deep breath in through your nose and then blow out the breath through your mouth. Repeat three times.*

2 *Imagine yourself standing on a beautiful beach. Look around you and admire the view.*

3 *As you look out to sea, watch the water moving in … and out … in … and out … Enjoy the movement of the sea.*

4 *Hear the birds singing above you.*

5 *Feel the water lapping gently around your feet.*

6 *Feel relaxed now.*

7 *Feel calm and peaceful.*

8 *Feel totally at ease.*

9 *Enjoy the relaxing sensations of being on the beach.*

10 *Become aware of a beautiful energy surrounding you and feel joy as the energy gets stronger. Enjoy the sensation of this total, unconditional love, flooding through your body.*

11 *Become aware that you are no longer alone. The energy comes from your own dear Guardian Angel, who is now standing in front of you. Smile in greeting as your loving friend steps forward.*

12 *Your Guardian Angel holds you gently and you feel excited at the opportunity of connecting with a familiar companion. You recognize this love and remember that your angel is always with you. You know inside that you have met many times before and will meet again. Take a moment to assimilate this information.*

TIP

Have a glass of water ready so that you can have a drink as soon as you come out of your meditation. If you prefer a hot drink, make one in advance and keep it in a flask at your side.

13 *Make a mental note of your angel's appearance. If you wish, ask her name.*

14 *Sit down together and take a few moments to speak with your angel. Ask any questions you may have and wait as your angel answers you.*

15 *Now your angel is ready to pull away, and you hug goodbye. Your angel reassures you that you can come back to this place at any time and meet face to face again if you wish. Your angel is always close by. You know that you will communicate in this way again, over and over, and each time your contact will become stronger and clearer. You are happy and contented, you feel at peace.*

16 *You are now totally relaxed and refreshed. When you are ready, begin to come back into the present. Open your eyes in your own time and be aware of your surroundings. Look around and orient yourself back into your body.*

MEDITATION NOTES

Once you are wide awake after the meditation exercise, make some notes about what you have experienced in the journal in Chapter 8. You'll find recording your experiences will help you to get better and better. Practice the exercise—a lot!

Connecting with Angel Guidance

Guardian Angels regularly reach out to their human charges.
Our days are so busy that it's easy to miss their signs. Our minds are full
of internal chatter and we simply don't hear what they are saying, but
they are always around and we can learn to tune in to communication
from our celestial messengers.

By slowing down your mind, relaxing so that you are almost day-dreaming, you'll find it easier to pick up your angels' signals and they, in turn, will find it easier to reach down to you. Relaxing and finding time for contemplation is like doing a waking meditation. Try the following simple exercise.

Guardian Guidance

Angel contact is easier by water. We don't really understand why. Perhaps it's simply that humans are more relaxed when close to water. Ideally, take a stroll along the seashore, a riverbank, or alongside a gently running stream. If all else fails, take a shower and do this exercise there—surprisingly, it will work just as well.

TIP

Try to do the water exercise when you are already feeling relaxed.
You'll find you accomplish more. When you're tense or worried
about home or work matters, relaxing in this way will just bring
those concerns immediately to mind. You can still push through
these feelings but it may take longer to do so. Work on the exercise on
a day when you have plenty of time and don't feel rushed.

With your eyes closed, walking or standing, take a moment to soak up the energy in the atmosphere around you. Running water produces negative ions in the air. Scientists believe it makes you feel happier, more energized, and better able to concentrate. It certainly helps you to feel better. Relax as you do so.

Now clear your mind. Concentrate only on the sound of running water. This might be the crashing of the waves, the sound of water hitting the shower tray, or the trickling of a mountain stream.

You might get a sense of peace or even feel a little "blissed-out." With practice, you may sense your angel is with you, or feel a message from your angel. Your Guardian Angel may take the opportunity of bringing you healing energies or directly communicate a sentence or two (usually angelic messages appear as ideas rather than individual words).

TIP

Keep your Guardian Angel in mind. You don't need to ask any specific questions the first few times you try this. Feel love surround your body as you breathe in and out. Just stay relaxed and happy and you'll draw more of this feeling toward you.

HOW WAS YOUR EXPERIENCE?

What did you experience during your water meditation? Did you sense your angel or even see her? Did you receive any messages? Make a note of your experience in the appropriate section in Chapter 8.

Communication Ritual

Your Guardian Angel longs to communicate with you. She is always with you, just close by, waiting to be noticed. If you'd like to receive guidance from your angel, why not write with her? You can handwrite your notes into a journal or, if you prefer, key your notes into your computer.

1 *Start by preparing your space and mind. Create a tranquil and relaxing room by placing some fresh flowers on the table or desk next to you. Maybe open the window to let in some fresh air.*

2 *Light a candle. Blue is a great color for communication and ritualistically opens your communication session. Blow it out at the end to close the session.*

3 *Play some soothing and relaxing music.*

4 *Have your notebook ready—I like to use a roller-ball pen as the words flow more easily—but if you prefer, sit at your computer and prepare your angel letter that way.*

5 *Angelic language, when it comes, can seem "flowery" and old fashioned to us. Just go with the flow. Start off by writing a sentence or two at the top of the page. Something like:*

TIP

You might prefer to use a gold or silver pen to make the experience feel magical, or just use your favorite pen.

My dear angel, I welcome contact with you and look forward to receiving your words of wisdom. Thank you for reaching out to me …

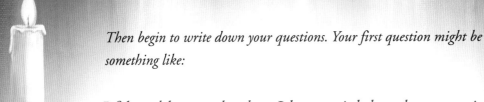

Then begin to write down your questions. Your first question might be something like:

I felt sad last week when I lost my job but that sensation was followed by a more peaceful feeling and I wondered if the contact was from you, my angel?

6   *The trick is to write down your reply immediately. If you are concerned that no answer will come, write the comforting and supportive answer that you know the angels would write to you if they had replied. Their reply might go as follows:*

Beloved, I am always with you in your time of need.

Work quickly with your questions and answers. Don't stop to think. With practice, you'll find that the answers come more quickly. You could try meditating first of all to see if this strengthens the response. Expect your Guardian Angel to use phrases and words such as "dear one" and "my love." The words that you think your angel might say will soon be replaced by words that flow from your fingers. You'll know you have connected with your Guardian Angel and she is communicating with you.

7   *Once you have finished, blow out the candle and thank your angel. You can write thank you in your text.*

8   *The next step may seem surprising. I want you to close your document or put away your notes without reading them! Don't peek. After a few days, take some time to go through what you have written. I think you will be surprised and find the information more useful—and you'll doubt the message less.*

*"It is not known precisely where angels dwell—
whether in the air, the void, or the planets. It has
not been God's pleasure that we should be
informed of their abode."*

Voltaire (writer and philosopher)

You can easily create your own rituals if you want to. When you feel more confident, have a go. One of my favorites is to connect with my angels using visual means. Angel altars or shrines can be such fun and you can use them in so many ways. Let's have a look at how to do this next.

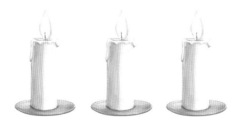

TIP

Your angel messages are always loving and kind, supportive and generous. If at any time you feel the messages are not like this, simply put down your pen, say thank you, and blow out your candle. Come back to your work on another day when you feel well and strong, and try again.

CHAPTER 6

Angel Altars, Displays, and Rituals

Altars can be used in many different ways. They are a wonderful focal point for your meditations and rituals— a place where you can be with your angels and enhance your connection with them. Discover how to create beautiful angel altars and displays in your home, and how to use them for specific purposes.

Using an Altar

The word altar has a religious connotation, but altars can be used in the home for non-religious reasons. In fact, not all of my readers think of themselves as religious; their belief in angels is more of a spiritual thing.

An altar, or shrine, is usually a raised table or shelf that has an arrangement of objects laid out on it as a point of focus. Your altar would typically be covered with an altar cloth and the items on it would include candles, flowers, and some sort of figurines or other magical objects. You can create an altar anywhere you want—on a coffee table in your living room, the windowsill in your kitchen, or even in the yard.

You can use your home altar as a permanent display to remind you of your belief in angels, something pretty to look at each time you pass by. I like to sit next to my altar—well, actually, I have several around the house—and meditate or read angel books. Create your display and then light a candle to dedicate the space. Use a small votive and let it burn down completely. Say the following words three times:

Angels dedicate my home, Gather in this space;
Bring your angel-energy to this time and place.

You can also infuse aromatherapy oils around or on the table. Specialist stores sell angel sprays—aromatherapy oils mixed with spring water and fixatives to stop them going moldy. You can buy special blends to energize and uplift the space as well as make it smell gorgeous! Alternatively, use an oil burner and add one or two drops of your favorite oil. Here are my favorites for angel work:

* *Lavender Fresh, natural, and good for lifting your room and your own vitality.*
* *Rosemary Cuts through negativity and is cleansing.*
* *Frankincense Brings the angels close, which is great for meditations.*
* *Rose The scent of roses is often noticed when people see or sense angels, so it is perfect for altars, since you are actively trying to attract your Guardian Angel's presence.*

Dedicate your Altar to a Purpose

Your altar isn't just a pretty display (although it could be). You can use it as a point of focus for rituals if you like. Many people report that over time their altar spaces seem to gather a wonderful angelic aura around them. It makes sense, after all.

When you see your display, you think of the angels and feel uplifted. That energy begins to gather in this area, and it's a shame to waste it. Here are some fun ideas:

* *Add photos to your altar to send that loving energy to family and friends.*
* *Create an angel altar for a special occasion, such as a birthday or Easter, and decorate it accordingly.*
* *Create an altar for a particular intent (a wish or hope). If you want a new car, why not decorate your display with appropriate images? If you long for a fabulous holiday abroad, include framed images of exotic landscapes of your choice. The angelic presence will help to reinforce your desire and bring it to fruition.*
* *If you want a change of career, look for suitable images to illustrate your aspiration and add these, too.*
* *Design an altar dedicated to a friend or family member, or a recently passed over loved one, by adding an object that belongs to the person, items that remind you of him or her, or letters, greetings cards, and photographs of happy times.*
* *Dedicate an altar to a beloved pet, on this side of life or the next. You can buy animal angels—pet figurines with wings—via the Internet and from stores selling memorial items.*
* *Color theme your altar to match your décor or mood. Silver and gold (anything shiny) are very fashionable right now, or how about an altar in your favorite angelic or spiritual colors—pink, blue, turquoise?*

If looking at your altar makes you feel uplifted or excited, you know you're on the right track.

The Main Ingredients

Find an empty shelf or box where you can store objects especially for your displays. Here are a few of the basic items you'll need for any altar:

* ***Cloth*** As a way of honoring your choice and your arrangement, it's lovely to display your objects on a carefully chosen cloth. Of course, you can use anything that fits your home décor and there are no rules. I often use a sparkly scarf or a white embroidered tablecloth (a family heirloom). You could buy a small length of fabric to match your décor and hem it by hand or use iron-on hem-strips to neaten up the edges. I've previously used Indian cotton tablecloths, which come in wonderful designs and colors. I never pay much for items and always look in the reduced section at the store! You've probably already got numerous fabric items at home that would be perfect as altar cloths.

* ***Tray*** A tray is a great way of corralling your display objects together. It looks neat and if you need to use the table for something else temporarily, you can easily move the display. A tray also helps to stop objects going astray, and cats or children from tapping small crystals onto the floor. My young granddaughter loves to play with my crystals, so I have to be careful when she is visiting. Do make sure that any small objects are safe around the people in your life.

* ***Candle*** Traditionally, one or several candles are included in an altar arrangement. They bring light energy and form part of any ritual you may want to do. Light a candle to open your ceremony, and blow it out to close it. You can select from a wide variety of colors and scents or use several candles in glass jars. Keep matches or a lighter in a glass jar or lidded pot at the back of the display for ease of access. Alternatively, you could use battery-operated lights and plug-in lamps or fairy lights. If none of these are appropriate for your home situation, consider using mirrors or shiny objects to bring in light energy. Glitter, foil confetti, or Christmas tree tinsel will do. You don't need to spend much money. Gather together existing pieces

from around your home or search your local discount store, garage sale, or thrift store for bargain buys.

* **Angel figures** Since our altars are going to be angel focused, you'll want to include something to represent angel energy and intervention. Look for carved angel figurines in wood or crystal, ceramic molded angels, or soapstone angels. You might like to build a collection as there are so many different types. Mine come from all over the place. Some are gifts from fans, some I buy new, but many come from thrift or resale stores. I adapt them to suit my personal style. You can use matching pairs, add one tall angel at the back of your display, or create a display of several angels in different sizes.

* **Crystals** Like the other objects you include, these will be personal to you. My favorites include Rose Quartz, Clear Quartz, and Amethyst. I like crystal clusters—crystals with points to focus that angel energy—and tumbled stones. These are crystals with the rough edges smoothed away, which double up as meditation tools that you can hold in your hand. It's always best to select your crystals personally. The ones you order off the Internet never seem the same to me. You'll want to feel an affinity to the crystal, an energetic connection that you can find only by hand-selecting the crystals you like and want to work with. You need to touch them if at all possible! Look out for rock and crystal shows in your area.

* **Natural objects** When you're out for a walk, look for things you can include in your displays. You could add pine cones, nuts, shells, or smooth-edged pebbles. How about gathering twigs, dried seedheads, or a few wild flowers?

* **Something green** I like to keep my altars fresh and alive by including flowers or a green plant. I favor white for most altars—it seems right for angel work—but you can change the colors depending on the seasons. Orchids are glamorous, daisies are very countrified and magical (they keep the naughty fairies away), and a green pot plant will last for ages, making it economical, too.

Laying Out an Altar

*A dining table, a coffee table, or any other flat surface
is fine as a base for your altar.*

Lay your cloth on the top, or use two, if you like, a big cloth underneath and something pretty or sparkly on the top. Place the largest objects at the back (plant, flowers, or tall angel figurine), and smaller objects toward the front, including candles, crystals, and natural objects. Keep candles away from other items so no fires are started.

Keep the display fresh and clean, changing the flowers when necessary. Choose different ones each time and change it all around or introduce new objects. You could keep your angel cards here, too, or a pile of angel books artfully arranged.

Glamorous coffee-table display

Did you know that whole blogs are devoted to arranging and styling, and particularly to coffee tables? Your coffee table can set the tone of the whole room, so this is the perfect place for a little angel altar.

* *Pile a group of angel books to one side of the table, largest at the bottom and smallest on the top (or have two piles if your table is wide enough). Between three and five is about right. Make sure the book on the top of the pile has an attractive cover. Either select books in colors that match your room or introduce accessories to match the books on the table—a pillow, a candle, or a bunch of flowers.*

* *Add a finishing touch to the top of the books—I love a glass paperweight, cut like a diamond. A little "sitting angel" in white or gold would be lovely. Anything shiny in gold or silver will make your display look glamorous, but keep it simple or architecturally in shape. A large shell is perfect or a large crystal. Why not spray paint an angel you already have to match your arrangement? You can buy mirror shine paint from the do-it-yourself store.*

* *Place a square or rectangular tray on the other side of the table. White, black, gold, and silver (or mirrored) are very fashionable right now, or spray paint an old tray to match your décor. Many angel books come in pink, lilac, or blue, so these would be perfect colors for your tray. Look around your home for items you can spray paint for your display.*

* *For height, add a pot plant or vase of flowers. Bear in mind that the wider the vase's base, the greater the stability. Some pebbles in the bottom of a clear glass vase look good and will help to stop it tipping over. If not clear glass, make sure the vase matches your display.*

* *Next add a candle—a jar candle is perfect and why not make it scented? Look for gold, silver, black, white, or a bright pop of color. You can make your own votive holders by cutting out an angel picture and sticking it to the outside of a short drinking glass. Add glitter or angel-cut foil confetti for sparkle.*

* *Finally, place a pretty box with a lid on your tray. I have several with angels on—even a wooden box with the word "angel" carved in it. This is the perfect place to hide your remote control, or a pack of angel cards so they are always handy. If you prefer, an open bowl with a pack of smaller angel cards would also be lovely.*

KEEPING A RECORD

What did you use to create your coffee-table display?
Draw it or take a photograph and keep it in the appropriate
section of Chapter 8.

Seasonal Angel Altars

If you are lucky enough to have the space to create permanent displays, you'll still want to swap things around from time to time—dust doesn't make for a well-cared-for look! One of the best ways to change your altar is to theme your displays by season. I'm always looking for excuses to create new displays.

* **Spring** *Start with an appropriate picture and prop it at the back of the display. Add your angel—color coordinated, if possible, or use white, which is always right. You might want to add a flowering bulb in a pot and something else to represent new birth, such as a photo of a family baby, some fluffy yellow chicks from the stationers, or a toy rabbit. Write the following words on a piece of paper, in gold ink if you can: "Angel Spring Energy Altar. Dedicated to New Life." Place the paper under your candle holder—or write the words on card and prop it up on the display—and light your candle. Sit close by. Select some angel cards from your pack or simply meditate for a while. When you've finished, blow out the candle.*

* **Summer** *This is a time of plenty. Work with the colors of sweet peas, the most glorious of all scented flowers—white, pinks, purples, and blues. Use this as an inspiration for your cloth and maybe use a piece of flowery fabric for your base. Add candles in summer flower scents and colors and surround your angel figurine or picture with matching crystals. Alternatively, gather your crystals together in a cut-glass bowl, or arrange them in a spiral pattern on a small round mirror. You can buy mirrors the size of coasters as a base for your candles—one of these would be perfect. Add a tall vase of bright, scented blooms. Write the following words on a piece of prettily decorated writing paper, or a flower-decorated notecard: "Angel Summer Energy Altar. Dedicated to Abundance." Frame the paper*

or prop your card up on the display. Take some time to sit and read by your altar. Enjoy the sunlight filtering through the window and browse through your angelic literature.

* *Fall* Orange, red, gold, and brown signify the fall, so look for cloths and candles in these colors. Include a matching crystal for energy, such as Red Jasper or a lovely brown Tiger's Eye, and flowers or leaves in deeper shades to match your display. A gold angel would be perfect for this arrangement, but you could also sprinkle around some angel confetti (gold-stamped foil in angel shapes). Add any seedheads and nuts that you have collected and

maybe burn some fruity smelling oils. Write out your dedication on a piece of orange or red paper, if you can get it, or use orange or red ink or pencil on white paper: "Angel Autumn Energy Altar. Dedicated to Closing Doors." (Ready to open new ones!) Sit down nearby. Take a notebook and write a little note to your angels. Thank them for everything they have done and describe how you would like to communicate with them over the coming months.

* ***Winter*** *The colder months bring their own beauty. A winter angel altar decorated with a multitude of candles can be stunning. You could also include indoor fairy lights—some flicker on and off—and this is a fabulous way of bringing a little enchantment to your display. I once had a Christmas-tree angel that was perfect for this type of arrangement. She had a gorgeous jacket and matching hat with fake-fur leopard print—my type of angel! Our local garden centers are full of different kinds of angels, and, of course, you can always decorate your own, if you are so inclined.*

Write your dedication on a piece of parchment-type paper, roll it up, and tie it with a ribbon, like a scroll: "Angel Winter Energy Altar. Time to Sleep, Time to Grow." Snuggle up in your favorite chair under a blanket, wearing comfy clothes, and stare at the candle flames as you relax and commune with your angels.

TIP

Your altar is meant to be exciting. If you begin to get bored with your display, it's time to adapt it by adding or taking something away. It might be enough to bring in fresh flowers, but sometimes the best thing to do is clear everything away and start afresh.

These are just suggestions of course. You can adapt your altars to suit your personality and the things you own. Change the words as you see fit and dedicate your altars to whatever you want. If you use the Internet, search on the Pinterest site for inspiring images. I have my own altar page there with photographs that I have found inspiring. Several images are from readers, which I have posted in permanent residence on my angel website.

An Angel Altar Outside

Even a very small outdoor space is enough for you to create a permanent altar area.

A place for meditation and contemplation in the fresh air is a real luxury. You can arrange the whole thing in an area about five feet (a meter and a half) square! Let your imagination run away with you. Here are a few suggestions:

* *Some type of lighting is appropriate. Glass jars with little candles or votives are atmospheric, or you could string up some outdoor fairy lights in the trees or on surrounding fences or walls.*

* *A bench, chair, or log to sit on is good. You'll feel drawn to sit for a while and relax, especially on sunny days. This is the perfect space to commune with your angels. Face your chair toward your altar or display.*

* *You'll want some sort of focal point. An angel statue or figurine is the obvious choice and you'll find a wide selection to suit all wallets at your nearest garden center. If you're craft-oriented, why not make something of your own?*

* *A raised platform is great for displaying a few objects. A slab or plank laid on bricks or boulders is sufficient. This will be your main altar. You could use a small outdoor table if you prefer, or decorate a large barrel or pot in which you could also grow a few herbs.*

* *Gather some pebbles from the seashore. I have some heart-shaped stones that I've collected over several years, which I love. Alternatively, build a collection of rocks or crystals. Remember to keep small objects away from young children for safety's sake.*

* *Theme your altar by decorating it with seasonal objects. How about a pile of pine cones or jar of seedheads? Fill plant pots with fresh flowering plants—scented white flowers are especially beautiful—and a birdseed dish filled with a collection of beautiful seashells would look gorgeous.*

* *Another theme for your meditation space is color. Imagine everything in pink or blue! Lovely!*

I have numerous angel figurines around my yard. One sits on the edge of a birdbath, which helps to create a whole themed angelic garden. If funds allow, a large piece of quartz crystal really energizes your outdoor space. You might be able to highlight your favorite objects using lighting. Feeding the birds or planting butterfly-friendly plants will help to create a tranquil feeling. A running-water feature would be fabulous. Your space is about energy—not money, so build your altar or angelic meditation space over time and add plenty of natural objects.

If you like crafts, you might enjoy painting on pebbles. Include suitable words, such as peace, joy, love, and then varnish your pebbles to protect them from the elements. Keep moving items, and adding and taking away. Scented herbs are a special treat—plant them in pots next to your meditation area.

Ritual blessing for your outdoor space

Rituals can be helpful in reinforcing your will or intent. Light a white candle in your new magical space. Imagine that a white angelic mist or cloud is surrounding your angel garden. This light is full of loving angel energy. Say three times: "Angels bring your love to fill this magical space of my creation, meditation, and contemplation. May I ask that you communicate with me here? Welcome dear ones." Relax or meditate while your candle burns away.

TIP

If you don't have an outdoor space, never mind. Move a chair in front of a window, surround yourself with plants and an indoor water feature, and adjust the lighting. Work on an outdoor plant display—maybe a windowbox or hanging basket, or something you can look at through the window. You could add clip-on angels, butterflies, or crystals, or hang your windchimes or bird feeders right onto the window frame! If this is too difficult, wind silk flowers around your headboard and glue on some plastic angels. Attach fairy lights and you're there!

An Angel Altar for Connecting with Your Ancestors

In many cultures, people remember lost relatives by performing rituals relating to these loved ones on the other side.

My books are full of stories of loving family members reaching out from the afterlife to assist those still here on Earth. The Native Americans performed various rituals; especially those relating to health and healing. Other rituals were used as a way of honoring the family and the tribe as a whole.

"Día de los Muertos" is a Spanish phrase meaning Day of the Dead. It's a yearly celebration performed in Mexico, where family members create altars in their homes to remember those who have passed before. Flowers, particularly marigolds, are important in the celebrations. Families display the favorite food of the deceased on their altars and many people make sweet treats shaped into skulls and skeletons, which they give as gifts or display on their altars.

Creating an angel ancestor altar

Start by covering a table, box, or mantelpiece with a white cloth, scarf, or sheet. I like to use an heirloom cloth as a way of bringing me closer to my loved ones. Then you'll want to gather together a few special objects to display. Arrange them in a way that pleases you.

* ***A white candle*** *Look for one you can leave burning safely in a jar.*
* ***Flowers*** *Fresh are perfect. Choose bright colors, like the Mexicans use—red, yellow, and orange. You can display your flowers in a vase or float flower heads in a dish of water. Wild flowers are also suitable. How about arranging flower heads in a pattern around your photographs?*
* ***An angel*** *This might be an angel figurine, a piece of angel jewelry, or perhaps a picture on a birthday or Christmas card.*
* ***Photographs of the deceased*** *You can include one particular loved one or photographs of several different people.*
* ***Mementoes*** *A few relevant trinkets or inherited items connected to your loved ones would be good.*

Ancestor ritual

Light your candle and sit close by it. In your mind, call to your Guardian Angel and ask that she take care of your loved ones in heaven. Know this is done. Ask that, when appropriate, your loved ones step forward to act as guardians and protectors, too. Give permission in your mind for them to help you and watch over you. You may see your ancestors step forward at this point. Smile and imagine loving energy flowing between you. Know that the spirit lives on and that your loved ones are always connected. When you've finished, blow out your candle.

TIP

For Mexicans, this is a special day in their calendar. It's about remembering loved ones with joy, taking time to connect with them in your heart. Plan the altar as the center of a family get-together. Keep the occasion loving and fun, and enjoy spending time with people you love on this side of life at the same time as honoring the deceased.

CHAPTER 7

True Stories of Angels in our Lives

I love to hear about my readers' true stories of angelic connection. I feel closer to my own angels and guides just hearing how these magical beings reach out to us in times of need. Some experiences are subtle and others very dramatic, but each has something special about it, and all stories are better for the sharing! Here is a selection of angel stories that I thought you would enjoy.

Wardrobe mountain

This shocking story luckily had a happy ending. It could have been very different!

"When I was five years old, I was into everything, especially climbing and getting into mischief. One day I decided it would be a great idea to climb the biggest mountain in the world, my parents' wardrobe. At first, everything seemed fine, but suddenly the wardrobe began to lean forward and I was on the falling end of it.

You hear people talking about things starting to happen in slow motion during a trauma or crisis, and this is exactly what happened to me. The weird thing is that from out of nowhere, my father appeared, or someone I thought was my father. My father was, and still is, very much alive. This figure appeared and grabbed me as well as somehow stopping the wardrobe from falling on me, both at the same time. He placed me very gently on the floor, and I said, 'Thanks, Dad.' He just smiled at me and then vanished, right before my eyes!

I believe now the figure was an angel disguised as my father, so as to not frighten me any more than I already was. I never spoke to anyone about it, and it wasn't until many years later that I mentioned it to my wife for the first time. I'd never forgotten it.

The second account was when I was about eight years old. Some friends and I were playing on a bench. We were being silly and

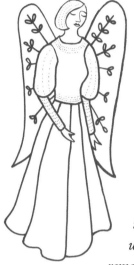

pushing each other but then one of my friends pushed me too hard and I fell backward toward a concrete path. Before I hit the ground, a hand reached out and caught my head, laying it gently on the ground. My friends kept checking but I had not a scratch, not even a lump on my head. I have no idea where the hand came from but it saved me from serious damage that day.

Then, when I was around 24 and married, an incident happened late one evening, around 11pm. My wife was in bed and I decided to meditate. I don't really remember any more other than that I seemed to come out of the meditation very quickly to see the most beautiful being ever. I was sitting on my sofa and this being was about ten feet away from me. The surrounding light was so bright, I couldn't see the stairs behind the apparition. Within this light was a being of such wonderment … I would say 'majestic' but that wouldn't even begin to describe what I was looking at. I felt like I was looking at serenity in its purest form. The being was female and had the longest, curliest golden hair I have ever seen. I couldn't see a face because the light was so bright and white. Yet even though it was so bright, it didn't make my eyes squint.

I remember just lying there thinking how beautiful she was, over and over. Then I sat up and she immediately disappeared."

Ian

Archangel Michael's sword

It's always helpful to remember that we can call upon angels to keep watch over our loved ones. This story shows that they listen and act upon our requests.

"One of my very best friends joined the Royal Marines as soon as we left school. We'd become friends at the start of secondary school (Grade 7 at junior high), but neither of us realized that as tiny babies (born a month apart), our mothers were friends and would meet regularly for coffee mornings, bringing us with them.

On his 18th birthday, he flew out to Iraq for six months. I was so worried about him that I prayed to the Archangel Michael, the warrior angel, to protect him while he was away. The next morning I was dashing around, getting ready to go to work, when I noticed something on the bedroom floor. I bent down to pick it up and was stunned to discover a tiny plastic bronze sword. There were no children or toys in my house, so to this day I have no idea where the sword came from. Of course, the Archangel Michael is always pictured with his flaming sword so, naturally, I took it as a sign that he was answering my prayers. I stood the sword against a photo of my friend and it's still there today.

Thankfully, my friend came back safely, but he'll always need protection with his choice of career. If I'm ever worried, I think back to that little sword and feel reassured."

Jessica

Feather on the roof

Angels can help when we're worried about hospital visits and other healing treatments. They were around for this family and left their favorite calling card for them.

"My husband David was in hospital undergoing an emergency spine operation and I was just preparing to visit him. Sitting on our bed, I was worrying about the outcome and decided to pray. Just at that moment I looked out of the bedroom window and found myself drawn to the roof of the garage. It was a very still day and to my amazement, bobbing up and down on the roof, was a brilliant white curled feather.

Right away I felt that my prayers had been answered and my fears melted away. I felt so peaceful. I'm pleased to say that my husband came through the operation safely and made a good recovery."

Michelle

"We are each of us angels with only one wing, and we can only fly by embracing one another."

Luciano De Crescenzo (writer, actor, director, and engineer)

Funny angel coincidence

Angels do love to bring us signs using coincidences, and this story is the perfect example. It's also quite funny! The story came to me in a letter from a woman who'd attended one of my angel workshops. I've left the letter in full here.

"Hi Jacky, just wanted to share with you what happened today. I noticed a beautiful white feather on my daughter's windowsill; it was nestled between her teddies. I smiled as I knew it was a confirmation that the angels were with us after going on your angel course (I'd never left my daughters overnight before).

Tonight I had a 'date night' with my husband and we went to a lovely pub serving great food. We were sat next to a table with two couples—two women and their husbands. At one point the two women popped to the ladies and were gone for some while. During that time I told my husband about your angel course, the angel feathers, and finding the white feather in my daughter Emma's room earlier in the day. We also talked about some other things and then the ladies came back to their seats. One of them spotted a feather on her seat and held it up in the air. It was a beautiful white feather like the one I'd seen in Emma's room. She said to her companions, 'Look, it's a sign angels are around …'

I couldn't believe what I heard! We had literally just been talking about angel feathers and I had to restrain myself from jumping in on their conversation! I felt as if the angels were laughing around us, like they were enjoying their little cosmic joke. Obviously, I'm very grateful for their presence and for giving their assurance. I'm so glad I came on your course!"

Jacquie

Fan angel

Angels can be in any country and make their presence known in numerous surprising ways, like in this next story.

"I was on holiday in Tunisia with my mom and dad when I was 13. We spent the day at the beach. It was an extremely hot day and my mom felt faint. What we hadn't realized was that she had heatstroke. We were trying to get across a busy road to get back to our hotel, but as we tried to cross the road, my mom started to collapse, and by the time we reached the other side she was unconscious. A few people were throwing water over her to help her come round and then out of nowhere an old woman dressed in black appeared and started fanning her with a big piece of cardboard. Mom finally came round.

Dad and I were so relieved and looked up to say thank you to the woman but she had disappeared. She was nowhere to be seen and a massive stretch of high wall surrounded the hotel so there was nowhere she could have gone. We looked around for a while but there was no one anywhere that looked like her or was wearing the same clothing. After that, we firmly believed that Mom was visited by a Guardian Angel. There seems no other explanation at all."

Zoe

Calling 222 angels

Some people see strange number patterns relating to angels—
11:11 is a common sign and is known as a "wake-up call" or a call to
recognize yourself as a spiritual being. Some see the repeating numbers of
222 as angelic, meaning that everything will be okay. Sherryl
sees angel numbers all the time.

"My angel signs are 2, 22, 222, or 2222. My dad had been seriously ill in
hospital and I had felt the angels draw around him. I didn't quite know
whether they were coming for him or offering healing, so on the way home
I asked my angels for a sign that he would be okay. As I pulled up at the
traffic lights, which were on red, a car pulled in front of me. The number
plate was 222 DAD, and I knew right away that he would be okay!

Just after this, it was my 42nd birthday. I had a wonderful day and as I
went to sleep, every time I turned over on my side, I heard a noise that
sounded like windchimes gently swaying but more magical. It was like
nothing I had ever heard before, but it just got louder and louder. Then I
felt something happening in the room, as if someone was there. It was
weird because I opened my eyes a little and could see three shadowy beings
standing at the bottom of the bed. Someone was pulling at my body,
which was raised very high. It felt arched and then I fell backward as if
something had been released from my body, and the room just filled with
pure love and tranquility. It felt so serene and I remember thinking that if
this is what death is like, I have nothing to fear. I awoke straight after this
and looked at the clock. It was 2.22am."

Sherryl

Angels changed my life

Sometimes angel visits are understated—gentle little reminders that our angels are around—and numbers and feathers come under this heading. Occasionally, though, their interaction is dramatic, as in this story.

"Back in 1988, driving through central London on my way to my first day at work as a TV announcer, live on air, I was crossing a junction when I was broadsided by a car racing off the lights. My car flew into the air, and everything happened in slow motion. I watched the sky going past as I turned my head to look left in the direction the car had hit me, and I recall thinking, 'Oh no! The car's rolling. Is this it? Am I going to die?'

The car landed on its side and all the windows shattered. Experts suggest I must have hit my head on impact, but I don't remember landing at all. After what seemed a few moments, but might have been minutes, I thought I'd better try to wriggle my feet and hands to see if they worked. They did, so I clicked off the seatbelt and, shaking, pulled myself into an upright position, with my head poking up through the passenger side window. Broken glass poured off me like water in a shower, and yet there was not a scratch or graze on me.

This was my 'wake-up call.' Before this, I had no awareness of things metaphysical, or angels. I had also been told I could not have children yet at the time of the accident I was four months pregnant with my only child. I had no idea until I visited the doctor in the aftermath of the accident.

My daughter is my miracle. Healing the trauma to my neck and back introduced me to osteopathy, alternative therapies, and eventually to Reiki healing and angels. I now work as a bodywork therapist, psychic advisor, and angel-therapy practitioner, so the accident, horrific though it was, changed my life and set me on a new path."

Erica

SHARING YOUR STORIES

True life angel stories are life changing to experience and even read about. I've gathered many of them in my books. If you've recognized or remembered experiences of your own after reading the stories in this book, why not make a note of them for future generations to read? Pass the magic on.

CHAPTER 8

Your Own Angelic Journey

Throughout the book, where you see the pen icon, you have been guided to fill in the journal that follows. This is to help you keep a record of your angel experiences and chart your personal angel journey. Continue to keep records either within these pages, or separately if you prefer, and enjoy the magical angelic relationship that unfolds.

When did you first hear about angels? And what sparked your interest? Perhaps, like me, you recall instances of angels from school or nursery, or maybe a special person in your life sparked your interest? Have you talked about angels with friends or loved ones at important times in your life? Write about it here.

Do you have loved ones in heaven who act as Guardian Angels now? They may be people you know or older relatives or family members whom you have never met. Have you ever felt them close, or perhaps living relatives have called upon them for assistance and protection? Which spirits would be taking care of you on this side of life and why? Make a few notes here.

Have you had times in your life when you felt that an angel intervened or kept you from danger? You might have been driving in a car or perhaps found yourself in a frightening situation. Write up what you remember here.

Which angel-themed television shows or movies have you seen? Make a list of those you have watched or would like to see. Ask friends for recommendations. Tick them off once you have watched them.

☐

☐

☐

☐

☐

☐

☐

☐

☐

☐

☐

☐

☐

☐

☐

☐

☐

☐

☐

☐

☐

Where are the angels hiding in your home? Are they on T-shirts? Mugs? Sitting on shelves or perhaps decorating notebooks? Make a list of some of the angels in your life. If you love angels, you'll be surprised at where they hang out.

Thousands of songs have been written with the word "angel" in the lyrics. What are your favorites?

Do you own angel music—music that represents the sound of the angelic choir? Make a note of your albums here, or any you would like to add to your collection.

What did you use to create your coffee-table display? Draw it or take a photograph and include it here.

Make a list here of angel books you've read, owned, or
borrowed, and any you'd like to purchase.

Do you have any of the following items in your magical toolbox? Tick them off if you do, and make a list of other items you'd like to have in your life. I'm sure your angels will help to bring them to you.

Angel notebook or journal for recording experiences ☐

Angel cards ☐

Angel boards ☐

Angel pendulum ☐

Angel crystals ☐

Statues or figurines ☐

Home-made objects ☐

Other magical angel items ☐

After your first angel meditation, write down what you

experienced here. Add to your notes as you do the

exercises again.

Did you meet your Guardian Angel? Write down what you experienced here and add to it each time you perform the meditation. What did your angel look like? Do you recall noticing eye color, hair, or clothing? Did you recognize her? Did your angel give you her name? What questions did you ask and what answers did you receive?

What did you experience during your angel water meditation? Make a note of your experience here.

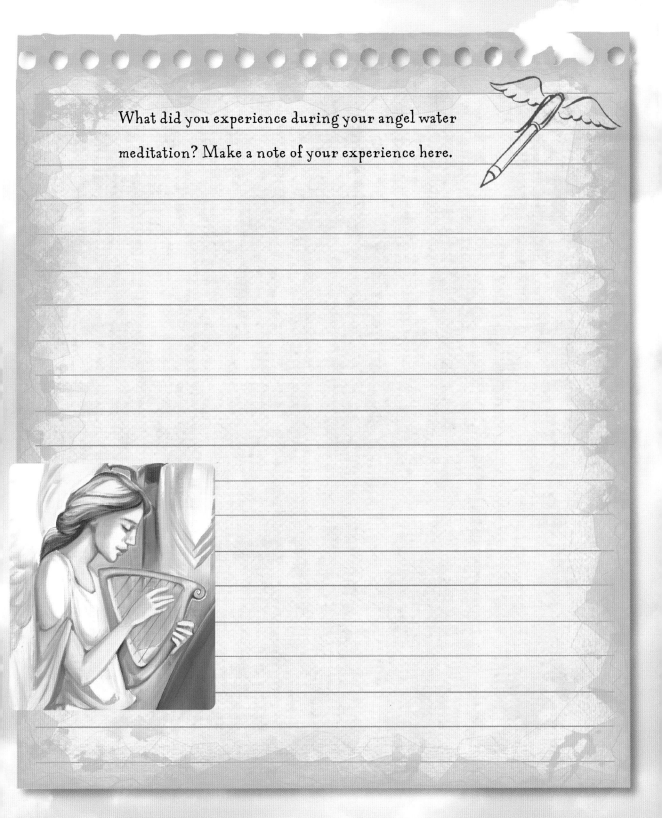

What are your favorite scents and why? Make a note of any oils you burn and keep a record of how you feel, or any experiences you might have when using the oils.

How would you like your Guardian Angel to contact you? Are you open to feather signs, coincidences, or maybe dreams? If you have your own ideas, write them here. Leave this note for your angels.

Dear Angels, I'd love you to show that you are around me by contacting me in the following ways:

Index

A

accidents 20–1, 58, 104–5, 112–13
affirmation cards 28, 31
affirmations 54
age of angels 17
altars 87–101
    connecting with ancestors 100–1
    dedicating 89, 100
    displays 88, 89, 90–3, 101, 128
    laying out 92–3
    outside 97–9
    seasonal 94–6
    using 88
ancestors, connecting with 100–1, 118
angel, definition 17
angel boards 31–2, 131
angel books 28, 32–3, 92, 130
angel cards 28, 30, 31, 92, 131
angelic choir 34, 63, 126
animals/pets 89
Apollyon 22
appearance (aspect) of angels 13–14, 22, 38–9, 136
appearance/arrival of angels see encounters with angels
archangels
    definition 16–17
    guidance from 51–7
    Michaelmas 22
    role 41, 51
Ariel, Archangel 14, 52
aromatherapy oils 33, 88, 95, 138
art 38–9
asking for help 42, 43, 46–7
aura 49
Azrael, Archangel 52

B

belief in angels 18, 36
Bible 22, 23, 36
books 28, 32–3, 92, 130
Buddhism 37

C

candles, altar 90–1, 92, 93, 94–6, 97, 101
cards 28, 30, 31, 92, 131
Chamuel, Archangel 52
cherubs 22
childhood memories 7, 116
children
    help from angels 53
    visits from angels 14–15, 20–1
Christian beliefs 36–7, 38
coffee table altars 92–3, 128
coin
    angel 43
    angelic gifts 63
coincidences 63–4, 108, 140
collecting
    angels 23, 28–33, 124
    feathers 68, 71
color, altars 89, 91, 92, 94, 97
communicating with angels 80–5
    affirmations 56
    angel boards 31–2
    angel signs 71, 140
    keeping records 136
    in writing 83–5
communication, help with 52
connecting with angels 56, 66, 74, 78–85
crystals 32, 63, 76, 91, 94–5, 98, 132

D

Day of the Dead 100, 101
daydreaming 16, 80
deceased relatives
    altar dedication 89, 100–1
    angels accompanying 46, 52, 64
    babies 22
    connecting with 100–1
    Guardian Angels 14–15, 46, 118
depictions of angels 13–14
discovering angels 7–9, 12–17, 18, 116

divination cards 28, 31

E

encounters with angels
    giving support 42–3, 104–5
    recording experiences 136
    seeing angels 16, 66–7, 105
    signs 62–71, 80, 110, 112, 140

F

fallen angels 22
family 53, 89
feathers 62, 66, 67–71, 107, 140
figurines
    on altar 91, 94–5, 97–8, 101
    collecting 28, 30, 132
    meditation 76
film depictions 26–7, 122
flowers, altar 91, 92, 93, 94, 97, 100–1

G

Gabriel, Archangel 22, 36, 52
gifts from angels 63
Greek beliefs 22, 37, 38
guidance of angels 45–7, 49, 51–7
guided meditation 77–9

H

halos 13, 38–9
Haniel, Archangel 52
healing 42, 48–50, 53, 70, 107, 109
help
    asking for 42, 43, 46–7
    from Archangels 52–3, 106
    protection 58–9, 104–5, 106, 120
    signs from angels 63, 107, 140
Hinduism 37
historical references 23
home, angels in 28–33, 124

Thank you for reading this book. It's been a pleasure to work with you. Don't forget your Guardian Angel is always by your side and she is just longing to work with you and be recognized. Talk to your angel every day and know that you will be heard. Your Guardian Angel loves you very much indeed.

Angel blessings

Jacky Newcomb
www.JackyNewcomb.com